TO THE BEST OF
MY RECOLLECTION

My Memoir

The Early Years

TO THE BEST OF MY RECOLLECTION

My Memoir

The Early Years

by

RANDY WILLIS

To The Best of My Recollection
My Memoir
The Early Years

Published by:
American Writers Publishing, LLC
PO Box 111
Wimberley, Texas 78676

www.threewindsblowing.com
512-565-0161
randywillisnovelist@gmail.com

ISBN-13: 979-8588449724

Library of Congress Control Number: 2024936205

Printed in the United States of America

PREFACE

This book is written for and dedicated to nine people: my three sons and six grandchildren. They are the joy of my life. Anyone else who would care to listen in is welcome.

DEDICATION

To my three sons
Aaron Joseph Willis
Joshua Randall Willis
Adam Lee Willis

And my six grandchildren
Baylee Coatney Willis
Corbin Randall Willis
Presley Rose Willis
Olivia Grace Willis
Juliette Rebecca Willis
Violet Jean Willis
and my future grandchildren

With gratitude and love

"Their strength of character has been demonstrated many times by how they treat people who can do nothing for them." —Randy Willis, aka Dad, Grandpa, Papaw.

"Go now, write it on a tablet for them, inscribe it on a scroll, that for the days to come it may be an everlasting witness." Isaiah 30:8

My Six Grandchildren are Presley, Baylee, Violet, Corbin, Olivia, and Juliette. I'd had them first if I'd known how much fun grandchildren were.

I've learned much from seeing the world through the eyes of my grandchildren. Jesus said, "Let the little children come to Me, and do not forbid them; for of such is the kingdom of heaven." Matthew 19:14

Introduction

Merriam-Webster dictionary defines happenstance as "circumstance especially that is due to chance."

My late friend, Texas Longhorn Football Coach Darrell K Royal, said, "Luck happens when preparation meets opportunity."

One of my favorite writers, literary scholar C. S. Lewis, wrote, "Hardships often prepare ordinary people for an extraordinary destiny." That quote inspired my trilogy, *Destiny*.

I was thirteen on November 22, 1963. Around 1:00 that afternoon, I walked from my art classroom under the Angleton Junior High football stadium. A very excited classmate, Robert Munson, stopped me between the cafeteria and gym and asked, "Have you heard the president has been shot?"

Darrell Royal was hand-picked to greet President John F. Kennedy when Air Force One touched down at Bergstrom Air Force Base, seven miles from Austin, at 3:15 pm on November 22, 1963. Coach Royal was tying his tie and then heading to the airport when he heard the tragic news on the radio that President Kennedy had been shot in Dallas.

On that same day, C.S Lewis died. Only two news outlets contacted his family about the details of the Christian author's death. *The New York Times* announced Lewis's death two days later, on November 24, 1963.

I believe our choices and the undeserved favor of the Lord, not luck, determine our destiny.

If there is a verse in the Book that would put my biography on a bumper sticker, it would be found in Joshua 24:13: "I have given you a land for which you did not labor, and cities which you did not build, and you dwell in them; you eat of the vineyards and olive groves which you did not plant."

Thank the Lord for His undeserved—unearned—unmerited favor called grace, for I have made many wrong choices.

My life is a story of triumph over tragedy and victory over adversity. And what to do when your whole world crumbles around you.

"For by grace you have been saved through faith, and that not of yourselves; *it is* the gift of God, not of works, lest anyone should boast." Ephesians 2:8-9

Randy Willis, ten months old, and his sister Johnnie
Ruth. October 1950. Home Longleaf, Louisiana.

TABLE OF CONTENTS
The Early Years

9

COWMEN

"The best men I've known have been cowmen.

"There's a code they live by—it's their way of life. It starts with an abiding reverence for the Good Lord.

"They're taught to honor and respect their parents and to share both blanket and bread. Their words are their bond, a handshake—their contract.

"They're good stewards of His creation, the land. They believe the words in His Book.

"Learn from these men—from their stories of triumph over tragedy—victory over adversity, for the wisdom of others blows where it wishes—like a *Texas Wind*."
—Randy Willis

Josh Willis, future cowboy, with his Grandpa Jake Willis

RIDER IN THE SKY

"A Rider is coming on a magnificent steed, a white horse, I'm told.

"He knows all the brands and earmarks, for you see, He owns the cattle on a thousand hills.

"He will separate the goats from His sheep.

"If you listen carefully, you might hear hoofbeats, for you see, He's mounted even as I speak.

"Not even a Texas Wind can change the fact that He's coming—*coming again*!"

—Randy Willis

Daddy and Mama, and my future half-sister Marjorie.
Dinner on the Grounds. Longleaf Baptist Church
Longleaf, Louisiana. 1948, a year before I was born.

Mama, Daddy, and Grandma Lillie Willis
Our home in Longleaf, near Barber Creek
1948. The year before I was born.

The longleaf pine trees were tall giants, and it was difficult for a small boy to see their tops.

☆　　☆　　☆

CHAPTER 1
WHAT'S IN A NAME
LONGLEAF, LOUISIANA 1949-1954

Julian Willis married Ruth Lawson Duke on June 26, 1948.

The following year, two significant events would occur within two weeks of each other for Julian—only one for Ruth.

The first for Julian was when it was announced the undefeated Oklahoma Sooners, led by All-American Quarterback Darrell Royal, were to play the Cinderella team of the South, the LSU Tigers, on January 2, 1950, in the Sugar Bowl in New Orleans.

The second event of far less importance was the birth of Julian and Ruth's son 14 days before the Sugar Bowl. That was me.

On December 1, 1949, my mother passed her due date.

As Friday, December 16, arrived, the temperatures dropped to the mid-20s as a Blue Norther blew into Central Louisiana. The question on everyone's mind was, would there be a White Christmas? It snowed five inches 20 years before on December 22, 1929, three days before Christmas, but it had not snowed on Christmas Day since 1895 in this area of Louisiana.

Many hoped to see their first White Christmas, but not Mother and Daddy; they were concerned about the roads. If they stayed frozen, their Oldsmobile threadbare tires might cause the car to slide off Highway 165 on the drive to Hargrove Clinic in Oakdale.

15

People were shopping in Alexandria (Alex), 20 miles in the other direction, the week before Christmas. Mother prayed she would not go into labor until after the ice had melted.

Mama needed to consult her physician, Dr. Rigsby Hargrove, but it would have to wait until the temperatures rose above freezing unless she went into labor. Dr. Hargrove was the closest medical doctor. The Hargrove Clinic was 15 miles from Longleaf.

William Rigsby Hargrove, M.D., delivered me on a cold (mid-40s) but not freezing Monday night, before the stroke of midnight, at 10:55 pm on the 19th day of December 1949. Louisiana rejoiced, not because of my birth, but because LSU was playing Oklahoma in the Sugar Bowl.

Daddy asked his mother, Lillie Hanks Willis, if it would be okay to name me after his father and her late husband, Randall Lee "Rand" Willis. "Do you think he would have liked that?" Daddy asked.

Thus, my life began as a tiny 10-pound, 8-ounce boy. It was said to have been a 10-month pregnancy. The ordeal was too much for Mother—I would be her last child and Daddy's only child. She was 36. Daddy was 30. Everyone called me Rand or Randy after my grandpa.

My mother's four previous children were with her late husband, John Duke. He died in 1946. Daddy raised them as his own; I never considered them half anything.

On my birthday, I have never had to compete with the Sugar Bowl again. Now Christmas is another matter. Bah! Humbug! I know.

Fourteen days after my birth, on January 2, 1950, over 82,000 attended Tulane Stadium for the Sugar Bowl in New Orleans. The newspapers reported the final score as 35 to 0 in favor of Oklahoma, but I was too young to recall. The weather was more like early fall than winter, clear with a high of 70.

Years later, I became good friends with University of Texas football Coach Darrell Royal. He had no problem in 1994 remembering the score and every play in much detail over lunch in Austin on East 6th at Cisco's Restaurant.

Daddy's memory seemed to fail him when I asked about the game one night around a massive campfire at our deer lease near Llano, Texas.

My Dad, Julian "Jake Willis," Darrell K Royal, and my late pastor, JB Young in Wimberley, were the best men I've ever known, except for my three sons, Aaron, Josh, and Adam Willis, and my grandson Corbin Willis.

Hargrove Clinic
William Rigsby Hargrove, M.D.
Oakdale, Louisiana, circa 1957

I was born in this building.

17

Randy Willis and Darrell Royal. 1994
Lunch in Austin on East 6th at Cisco's Restaurant.
Miss Edith's handwriting is at the bottom of the photo.
Photo Credit Edith Royal.

CHAPTER 2
LOUISIANA RED DIRT ROAD
LONGLEAF, LOUISIANA 1954

M y childhood began on a Louisiana red dirt road. We didn't have much money, but I never noticed because no one else did either— at least those my family socialized with.

As a boy, we lived near Willis Gunter Road and Barber Creek in an area known as Longleaf, Louisiana. Barber Creek flowed into Spring Creek. Both were as cold as ice. They were our principal place for recreation, along with an occasional Dinner on the Grounds at Longleaf Baptist Church, where Mother and Daddy belonged.

In those days, you sat on the ground—no lawn chairs. The dinner began with a very long prayer for an always-hungry four-year-old boy. It was a chance for the church folks to visit, sing, swap recipes, kids have a sack race or two, and, most of all, eat.

19

Each of the dear ladies would bring their favorite covered dish. Oh my, the food was better than any 5-Star restaurant today. To this day, I've never heard a Baptist sermon about overeating—thank God. It was also where I began to love music. I still love those old hymns.

One day, when I was four, I ventured up the narrow red dirt road lined with longleaf pines to my mother's mother, Nina Hanks Lawson's house. Her home was just a mile on Willis Gunter Road and overlooked Barber Creek near the Old Willis Home Place.

I remember stopping to pick wild dewberries. Perhaps Grandma would be so happy to see me that she'd bake me a pie while I swam in Barber Creek or at least have a cookie from her giant Aunt Jemima Cookie Jar. No sooner had I arrived than Mama drove up in our old Oldsmobile.

Now, Mama didn't seem happy with me. Visions of her making a switch by slowly cutting it from a tree—I mean very gradually—and removing the twigs one by one flooded my mind.

The drama of her cutting the switch was always worse than her application of it to my "seat" of knowledge. But that did not occur that day, although I later wished it had.

She pointed to an old grey-haired, swarthy-skinned man driving a mule-drawn wagon down Willis Gunter Road. She explained, "Rand, that old man drives that wagon up and down these red dirt roads looking for little boys. He then puts them in a gunnysack and hauls them off."

She did not say where he took them. I did not want to know. To this day, I've never run away from home again.

When I first shared this story with my eldest son Aaron, he responded, "He was driving a wagon? Who'd you vote for, Dad, Lincoln, or Douglas?"

I seldom get to walk those red dirt roads anymore.

Yet, there is another road, perhaps even less traveled than the red dirt road I trod as a boy in my beloved Louisiana or even the one Robert Frost wrote.

Travel this road, if you will. It will change your life. It can alter your destiny.

My maternal grandmother, Nina Ruth Hanks Lawson, who lived on Willis Gunter Road, is the person I ran away to at age four.

CHAPTER 3
GONE TO TEXAS
CLUTE, TEXAS 1954-1960

We moved from Longleaf, Louisiana, to Clute, Texas, when I was four.

All I remember of the trip was stopping at the Stateline in Deweyville, Texas, to buy gas. The pouring rain awoke my sister Marjorie, and she awoke me crying because her paper dolls had gotten wet. Our Oldsmobile and trailer were not as watertight as those today.

Daddy had gotten a job at Dow Chemical in Freeport, Texas. A.J. Jeffers was the first from the Longleaf area to leave for a job at Dow.

Mr. Jeffers returned and encouraged Daddy and others to do the same. A. J.'s brother, Jimmy Jeffers, and Daddy's brother, Herman Willis, soon followed. We were all close friends in Brazoria County, Texas.

Every Sunday morning, Sunday night, and Wednesday night, we were at Temple Baptist Church in Clute. It seemed to me that everyone attended church.

On a Wednesday night, my mother could not attend, so I walked to church from our home on Coleman Street with my twelve-year-old sister Marjorie. I was only eight years old. I had no intention of that night being any different from any other. I cannot recall a word Pastor Bill Campbell said in his sermon. But I remember vividly another voice that spoke to my mind—my heart—my spirit. It was not an audible voice. It was a still, gentle voice, tender but ever so clear, telling me to go forward and accept Christ as my Savior.

I recall my response to the Holy Spirit as if it was five minutes ago. "Lord, I'm too shy. I would if my mother was here to go with me."

I felt someone touch my left shoulder. My sister Marjorie was sitting in the back row with her friends. She could not have seen my face, for I was seated near the front.

She said, "I'll go with you if you want me to." I immediately stood and walked with her to the front of the church and made my decision public.

I know you do not have to have an experience like that to be saved. Nevertheless, I'm so grateful for that experience; it has never left my mind or my heart.

Lillie Hanks Willis and Randy Willis

Every Sunday, we put on our "Sunday Best." Growing up under my mother's roof, I never recall missing Church Sunday morning, Sunday evening, and Wednesday nights.

Mother's first husband, John Duke, died, and she married my Dad four years later. Mother had four children with John Duke. Daddy fed us all three meals daily, clothed us, provided a home, and never complained.

Far left Ruth Willis (Mother) and her children: Johnnie Ruth Duke, Dorothy Curbelo (whom my parents raised), Jerry Duke, Buddy Duke, Marjorie Duke, and me, Randy Willis, headed to Temple Baptist Church in Clute, Texas.

Dorothy Curbelo had been abused at her home in Vidor, Texas, according to my mother's sister. She asked my Mother and Daddy if they would take her in and care for her. Mother and Daddy said yes. It saved her life.

When Dorothy moved in, I never noticed less fried chicken, my favorite, on Sundays after church or not enough

24

slices of dewberry pie. But I did notice Mother put less food on her plate. She said, "I've decided to lose a little weight."

Suppertime at our humble home, 519 Coleman Street in Clute, Texas, was the best "church service" I ever attended, for I saw the love of Jesus around our supper table.

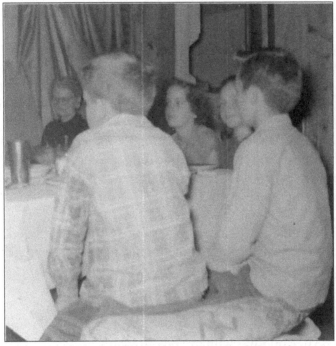

Randy, Buddy, Marjorie, Dorothy, and Grandma. Suppertime, 519 Coleman Street Clute, Texas.

No one's hands are on the table in the photo, for the prayer of thanks has not yet been given. Daddy would begin with, "Let's say grace." We never used "prepared" or repetitive prayers. The women were always served first.

During this time of joy and thanksgiving, we never discussed anything gloomy, such as politics or problems at

25

work, school, or church. There were no TVs turned on, TV dinners, or TV trays.

But, there were a few expected words. "Pass the Mayhaw Jelly and a hot biscuit, please," for example. The word please was part of every request. "Thank you" always followed when the butter was passed. You never reached in front of anyone. Yes, sir, no, ma'am, to your elders was a natural response. Good manners were not an option. You asked to be excused from the table.

And there was never a baseball cap or cowboy hat on in our home, much less around the supper table. I had no issue with this; it was natural, and I have admired it to this day, except for one detail. Daddy and Mother had attended a school of conservation for 10-plus years. A college of survival called the Great Depression. Therefore, you ate everything on your plate.

And that was fine, too, until one of my childhood's two most hated sentences was mentioned: "Eat your vegetables." I knew the day would arrive when the day's vegetable would be green peas. I hated the smell of green peas almost as much as I did liver.

After fiddling with my peas towards the end of the meal, I put a small spoonful in my mouth when Daddy looked at me. Oh, how I remember that look that always meant "Now." Within seconds, I threw up.

My sainted mother never served green peas again. She even stopped planting them in our garden.

Perhaps you may be wondering what my other most hated sentence was, "Bedtime Rand (or Randy)," which

Daddy never mentioned twice, except once. The second mention was not with words.

Christmas 1956 519 Coleman Street Clute, Texas Left to right: Lillie Hanks Willis, Julian Willis, Ruth Willis, Randy Willis (on the floor), Buddy Duke, Jerry Duke, Marjorie Duke, and Dorothy Curbelo.

Mama and Daddy were the first to trademark a TV remote control, an "electric" ice cream maker, and many other inventions. And Hollywood's Ozempic. The first two they called Randy. Thankfully, I was later replaced by a new "electric" ice cream maker model named Mama's Grandkids.

The last one, Ozempic, is trademarked as work. If I hadn't been fetched up on farm and ranch, I probably would have dressed out at 400 pounds because of Mama's cooking. We had no clue what calories or carbs were.

After church, we had dinner (called lunch today). The evening meal was supper, not dinner. Mother's fried chicken was cooked in a cast iron skillet. The grease was not hot enough unless you could light a kitchen match in the grease.

Mother cooked pineapple upside-down cake in a cast iron skillet, too. In fact, there's not much she didn't cook in one.

Mama also cooked with a cast iron Dutch oven chicken and dumplings, Louisiana file gumbo, and turnip greens with a large slice of salt pork. I'm surprised I can get through a metal detector today at the airport.

Then came the best, homemade vanilla pudding covered with vanilla wafers. Mama never used instant pudding or anything else instant, except perhaps me. And the very best homemade vanilla ice cream hand-cranked.

After Sunday dinner, we sometimes watched TV. We rarely had time for that luxury during the week. Daddy had a TV remote control named "Change the channel, Randy." I was glad there were only three stations, ABC, NBC, and CBS. That was not as bad as going outside in the heat, cold, and rain and turning the TV antenna until we got a signal. Thank God the TV guide later reduced the channel surfing.

A TV station out of Houston would often play *He's Got The Whole World In His Hands* by Mahalia Jackson before a movie. It blessed me every time I heard it.

Randy Willis, age eight.
Clute Elem. 1957-1958

CHAPTER 4
SURFSIDE BEACH

When we arrived in Clute in 1954, we discovered two places different from anything near Longleaf, Louisana. The first was Surfside Beach on the Gulf of Mexico, only nine miles from Clute, and the second was Dow Park, a mere five miles by way of the tiny town of Lake Jackson. And the price was within our budget—free.

Surfside's warm salty waters were a welcome relief from Barber Creek's fridge waters near our Louisiana homestead.

Mama said the salt water was good medicine for my frequent bouts with poison ivy. Our Oldsmobile was not undercoated, so eventual rust was the downfall. Later, car washes had jets spraying salt and sand loose from under your vehicle. Until then, It was me and a water hose that we soon discovered was ineffective when our Oldsmobile got rust holes in the fenders.

Many years later, I mentioned to an Austin medical doctor who had been recommended a couple of my mother's home remedies, such as salt water for rashes and hot mustard plaster on your chest for pleurisy; he smirked. When I brought up Epsom salt enemas for constipation, he was appalled.

So, I found another doctor. Later, when I got my medical degree from the "University of Google," I discovered that Epson Salt was bad for one's colon due to the elemental magnesium. Enough of that lovely discussion. Sorry, Doc.

Surfside Beach, age four & Clute Elem. age six

Headed to Surfside Beach at age 18. My date said I must take a photo with her Poodle or she would not go with me to Surfside. I explained that cowboys don't care much for house pets, which was not true; I was tired of her "dog and pony show" and anxious to go. Patience has never been a virtue of mine.

She was not impressed. I could hear my Catahoula Leopard Cow Dog "Bob" howling in Heaven when she took this photo.

CHAPTER 5
DOW PARK

A gigantic forest of arching Live Oak and Elm trees draped with Spanish Moss shadowed our picnic tables for Dow's annual picnic in '56. A strangely shaped restroom with many angles and a giant screened pavilion added to my fantasy land experience.

Ruth Willis next to Lake Jackson
Dow Park circa 1955

Mother next to Lake Jackson at Dow Park 1955

Rich folks lived in the distance on the far side of the oxbow lake, Lake Jackson, carved from the Brazos River bottomlands.

April showers brought May flowers to the enchanting park that seemed like a dreamland to me as the fast-approaching summer was just over the Brazos River horizon.

I ate until I could barely walk. "How could any company making Saran Wrap afford this much food," I wondered. I preferred waxed paper. As a six-year-old boy, I was happy as a colt in clover.

Ruth Willis   Jake Willis

Dow Chemical Company Annual Picnic
Dow Park on Lake Jackson
Saturday, May 26, 1956

Dow Chemical Company Annual Picnic, Saturday, May 26, 1956. I believe I'm seated in between Mama and Daddy. I was only six. That's my brother Buddy in front of Daddy and Jerry in front of Mama. That may be my sister Marjorie, who is to the far left on the other table with the Jackson family.

Daddy pulled two cane poles from our Oldsmobile's turtle hull (trunk) so we could fish on Lake Jackson's banks. A few short steps from the picnic tables.

As always, Daddy lit a Camel Non-Filter cigarette. He first smoked during World War II when the government provided the cigarettes. Uncle Sam said they would help soldiers mentally and physically get through the war. And they were not harmful to your health.

Daddy and Me (age 5) 1955.
519 Coleman Street Clute, Texas

I broke my arm playing on a swing set. The only broken bone I've ever had. Daddy chain-smoked until his brother Herman, who was 11 months younger than him, died slowly of cancer from smoking. Daddy never smoked again and would not allow anyone to smoke around him; he lived to 75.

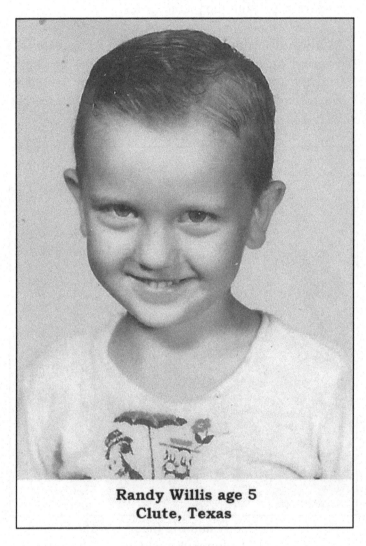

Randy Willis age 5
Clute, Texas

CHAPTER 6
THE KARANKAWA

The area to the west of Dow Park had been settled by Stephen F. Austin and his colonists. But others with darker skin were there long before the "Father of Texas." Artifacts from the Indigenous Karankawa reveal they were there as early as the 13th century. And lived between Galveston Bay and Corpus Christi Bay as far as 50 miles inland.

They were rumored to be seven feet tall, but archaeological studies discovered they averaged five-eight. The myth was a far better story when I went to camp.

As a boy, my Boys Scout Troup in Clute traveled a half hour west near Sweeny to camp at Camp Karankawa. It was one of the most memorable times of my life.

As a teenager, we worked cows on leased land by Daddy in the Brazos River bottomland near East Columbia, not far upriver from Dow Park. It was not for the faint of heart.

By the time Dow Chemical arrived, most of the area that had been the Jackson Plantation was gone with the wind. The plantation was destroyed by the Great Galveston Hurricane of 1900.

All that remained of the area's brief antebellum era was the beautiful horseshoe-shaped lake for which the town, Lake Jackson, was named and a few piles of bricks. Another large plantation owned by the Jackson family, Retrieve, had become a prison farm.

For me, it was paradise except for a few minor details: the heat, the humidity, the hurricanes, the snakes, and the mosquitoes. It's a small price to pay for a quality fishing hole.

The DDT pesticide-spewing fogging machines took care of the mosquito's plaque for a day or two. DDT was sprayed to kill mosquitoes, which were thought to carry polio. The best part was chasing the trucks with fogging machines and running through the dense fog. We were told it was safe, but I stopped when a whiff of the DDT caused me to drop to my knees, coughing. I never did that again or told my parents.

The government had us do drills in school, crawling under our tiny wooden desks to protect us just in case a nuclear bomb was dropped.

Someone said, "I'm from the government and here to help you." When I heard that, I wondered where the best place was to hide, perhaps with the seven-foot-tall Karankawa.

The Karankawa went without clothes and smeared themselves with alligator fat to repel the insects. That was funny to me as a boy. They were also cannibals. In fairness, they only ate their most hated enemies. I would have met them with Dunkin Donuts, Starbucks Coffee, and perhaps a few clothes from Brazos Mall's tall men's store.

Andrew Sansom, who headed Texas Parks and Wildlife when I produced the 75th Anniversary of Texas Parks and Wildlife Celebration at Garner State Park in '98, was from Lake Jackson.

I visited with Andrew the night before the main event at Garner, where I also produced for Texas Parks and Wildlife an event for its significant sponsors. It was a pickin' party on the banks of the far side of the Frio River from the campgrounds. The star-studded party is still available on YouTube.

Andrew Sansom added a closing remark at Garner about the woods nearby Dow Park, "That forest is unique to this hemisphere."

I wish I could take my grandkids to Dow Park today with a half-dozen cane poles. Maybe take a picnic lunch wrapped in waxed paper, too.

That dream will never be. Dow Chemical Company closed the 14-acre-plus park in the mid-eighties and sold it. The land ended up in the hands of private owners.

Dow Park on Lake Jackson. Lake Jackson, Texas

CHAPTER 7
SO, YOU WANT TO BE A COWBOY

After moving to Texas in 1954, we kept our home in Longleaf, Louisiana, and often visited to work cows with my Uncle Howard Willis and his sons in nearby Forest Hill. Even though we had moved, Daddy's cattle were still in Louisiana on the open range owned by colossal lumber companies. The open range surrounded my Uncle Howard's home for miles and miles.

I was always happy to return. I still am. The Longleaf pines and red dirt roads tend to become part of you. The Piney Woods will always be in my DNA. I long for the sweet-smelling perfume of the wood and the music from the wind whistling through the forest.

We had to hunt for our cows in the tall and thick Piney Woods before working them. It could be a monumental task to find them and then begin vaccinations, deworming, branding calves, and castrating bull calves. A rifle, rope, first aid, and water were not options in the woods. Neither were cow dogs and a cowbell.

Working cows in the Louisiana Piney Woods began by notifying neighbors to let us know if they had seen our herd. Once we got a lead, we set out on saddle horses with our Catahoula Leopard Dogs trained for this purpose. They are the only breed originating in Louisiana and are more focused and intelligent than any other breed I've ever known.

Catahoula Leopard Dogs hunting cows knew to listen for the sound of a cowbell worn around the neck of one cow in the herd. That combination was our only hope of finding and driving the cows through the dense and massive forest.

41

Louisiana's official state mammal, the Louisiana black bear, could be dangerous if she felt her cubs threatened. I never encountered one.

I did meet up with a hog, though. The colossal pig was not the kind of pig my granddaughter's pet at a petting zoo. He's a mean, scary, and dangerous Louisiana wild feral hog. As a boy, we saw a lot of them. They usually ran off when they heard us. Today, there are more feral hogs in Louisiana than people in Baton Rouge.

I shall never forget the day I followed our Catahoula cow dog, Jack, into the thick post oak while hunting cows on horseback. I was a 10-year-old boy hoping to be a cowboy like my Dad.

The chattering noise from the underbrush was unfamiliar to me but not to Jack. Suddenly, there was a loud growl as a wild boar began to charge Jack like a runaway train. Jack attacked him as if he was nothing more than a rabbit. The hog's tusk caught his belly and slit him from end to end as he jumped.

Jack, bleeding profusely, got up and, this time, went for the boar's hindquarters, clamping his jaws on his tail— refusing to let go and allowing me time to back off 30 or 40, maybe 50 feet as Daddy arrived.

With his lever-action Winchester 73, Daddy aimed and fired, hitting him in his thick skull, right between his eyes. The .44 caliber cartridge killed the boar just as Jack collapsed, and my horse bucked me off. Let me give you a heads-up: you don't want to be on the ground with an angry wild boar at any age.

Thankfully, the boar's tusk did not go deep enough to cut Jack's intestines or vital organs. Jack had nine lives and used one, or two, or maybe more that day.

I loved Jack and had wished before he would not behave with such reckless abandonment after a horse kicked him near our farmhouse in Texas. Jack lost an eye that day.

Thank the Lord, that wish did not come true. I might have gotten to where my decision at Temple Baptist would ultimately take me, albeit several decades before I had planned.

Daddy wrapped Jack with gauze and tape and carried him on horseback. He then cleaned the wound, coated it with coal oil and Pond's Extract, and dressed him in silver-coated bandages once we returned to Uncle Howard's house.

Daddy kept gauze with carbolic acid and wound dressings with iodin in his saddlebags. Grandpa "Rand" trained Daddy to dress wounds in horses, cows, dogs, and even ole cowboys if no people doctor was near.

Mama didn't allow "cowboy painkillers," such as whiskey. Uncle Howard and Daddy did not fare well on that "medical" remedy. In his younger days, Daddy could be as mean as a Louisiana wild boar on that treatment.

Daddy later used more modern treatments, such as combiotics (broad-spectrum, long-acting antibiotics), for possible infections. Veterinary Science has advanced significantly since those days, and that's understating it. Thank you to that "little school" in College Station.

We only had one horse that got lockjaw (tetanus). And we only had one other horse become infested with

43

screwworms. That was the most horrible sight I have ever seen in an animal or person—treatment involved removing the flesh-eating worms.

The screwworm eradication success still astounds me. Texas Governor Dolph Briscoe (1973-1979) played a significant role in eradicating the screwworm. He was from Uvalde and was a great Texan, if for no other reason than that. And there were many different reasons.

So you want to be a cowboy. Perhaps a cowgirl. One of my favorite John Wayne Westerns is *The Searchers*. I missed the part when John Wayne removed screwworms and doctored his horse with herbs, minerals, and poultices. Where's Natalie Wood mucking horse stalls in the livery stable? I haven't seen any horse manure on Main Street in the last 70 years in a Western. So, you want to be a cowboy? Then grab a shovel. And grab a pain killer, not Jack Daniels, Duke, but horse Liniment.

We always hoped and prayed for the best but were always prepared for the worst. There were no cell phones. It was a long ride home or town, even on a fast horse. To this day, I have a first-aid kit in my house, as well as pickups, tractors, barns, and saddlebags, and I do the same for my three sons, although none of them have ever requested it.

I learned that day why Winchester's Model 1873 was the favorite of ranchers, cowboys, lawmen, and outlaws over a half-century before.

An old rifle in the hands of an old cowboy was all the protection we needed that day and the Good Lord's favor. And a dog named Jack.

I loved that dog. I expect to see Jack again one day—when the lion lays down by the Catahoula Leopard Dog. Or was that the Louisiana wild feral hog—I hope not.

☆   ☆   ☆

Almost a dozen generations of my family have lived near Longleaf and Forest Hill, beginning with my 4th Great-Grandfather, Reverend Joseph Willis (1758-1854). Joseph swam the Mississippi River near Natchez 1798 on a mule, settled in Bayou Chicot, and moved to the Babbs Bridge area in 1828, known as Longleaf, Louisiana today.

I was not consistently working cows; I often rode my saddle horse through my family's neighboring property just for fun and exploring Hurricane Creek's banks between Butters Cemetery Road and Blue Lake Road near present-day Guillory Road, once William Prince Ford's Wallfield Plantation that I wrote about in my novels *Twice a Slave* and *Three Winds Blowing*.

45

During that time, I did not realize the significance of where I was riding and my ancestor Joseph Willis's connection to that land, James Bowie, William Prince Ford, and his slave Solomon Northup.

Once I found out, it would be the catalyst that would drive me to write and then rewrite.

☆　　☆　　☆

Randy Willis, age 11

Just finished lunch. I was waiting for my brother Jerry while comparing my Dad's horse to mine. His and Jerry's were always better. Well, that's okay.

46

CHAPTER 8
THE LAST PICTURE SHOW

As a boy between eight and twelve, I'd get to spend a few weeks at my Grandmother Lillie Hanks Willis's home each summer in Wardville, Louisiana.

Downtown Alexandra had a lot of movie theaters. The Don Theater was at 701 Bolton Avenue, and The Rex was at 1213 3rd Street (Lower Third and Jackson). I visited both. I never saw the inside of the fancy Paramount on Lower Third or the Joy Theater in a small corner building at 430 Murry Street.

Randy Willis, age nine

One summer, the Don Theater advertised that you could watch a Saturday monster movie matinee for six RC Cola bottle caps. I walked to the tiny corner grocery store at the corner of Westbrook Street and today's Bayou Maria Road in Wardville. Grandma's home was at 91 Westbrook Street, less than a hundred feet from the store. I found six RC Cola caps on the ground in front of the store. I was in "high cotton."

Grandma never owned an automobile or had a driver's license. When you are elderly and alone, you need a nearby grocery store, a bus stop, and, in Grandma's case, a Southern Baptist Church within walking distance. She had all three. Wardville Baptist was the farthest several hundred yards. But she would have walked it if it had been two miles.

I had six bottle caps and a bus stop at the nearby corner. All I needed was the roundtrip bus fare for the three-mile ride to downtown "Alex" (Alexandria for you Texans). Grandma gave me two dollars in quarters. That would cover the bus fare, a soda pop, a hotdog, and pay phone if needed with change to spare.

I was off to see *Frankenstein Meets the Wolf Man*. Bela Lugosi played Frankenstein's monster, and Lon Chaney Jr. played Wolf Man. Either one of them could scare a funeral up an alley.

I sat next to the aisle on the far-right side near the front. With an RC Cola, I was a loyal customer by then; I crunched on my nickel bag of popcorn with great anticipation. My budget wasn't large enough for one of my favorite candies, Milk Duds, Junior Mints, or Sugar Babies. I never cared for those candies from strange places like Hot Tamales or Turkish Taffy. The good news was they were all 100% natural refined sugar—none of that organic stuff.

The heavy red velvet stage curtain opened, dragging the floor. As the lights dimmed, all the kids began to scream. "Scaredy-cats," I said under my breath. As a 10-year-old follower of Roy Rogers and John Wayne, I was cool as a cucumber until a hand touched my left shoulder. I looked up, and there stood Frankenstein. I jumped as far as the row of seats in front of me would allow. My popcorn was all over the pretty girls seated in front of me.

I said, "I wasn't afraid." I knew they didn't buy my story by their expressions, but at least I had another nickel from Grandma to buy another bag of popcorn.

The good news was I hadn't noticed Wolf Man trolling down the opposite aisle. But I saw something else, even stranger, as I rushed to the lobby for a replacement bag of popcorn. There was a balcony full of kids, and none looked like me. I did not understand why they were up there. Perhaps they were in the cheaper three RC Cola caps seats. But that made no sense because they were all black.

Who were they, and why were they up there? The first question was answered as I left the theater. There was a second smaller entrance to the right of the primary access to the Don Theater. The sign on the glass door read, "Colored Only Entrance." The second question, why, has never been answered satisfactorily.

I visited the movies at the Surf Drive-in Theater on Highway 288 near Clute, Texas, several times. I never understood the rules for kids; my brothers Jerry and Buddy explained them to me. Kids could only enter if they were in the trunk or hidden in the back floorboard, and they remained silent as they drove in.

Surf Drive-In Theatre Highway 288 near Clute, Texas.

I vowed never to let a "picture show" scare me again. I broke that vow in 1967 at a movie entitled *Wait Until Dark* at the Lake Theater in Lake Jackson, Texas. Blind Susy (Audrey Hepburn) arms herself with a kitchen knife and turns off the lights—the famous jump scare scene caused half the audience to jump on the floor, except me, okay, maybe a little. Watch the scene on YouTube, and I dare you not to jump. I still do, and I know it's coming.

I drove my Dad's rusty old Ford pickup truck during those days. I was self-conscious about that. My first bonified real crush and date was lovely Betty McDaniel. She was way out of my league. I was smitten.

Betty's father and mother once escorted us to a foreign country to see a movie. The foreign land was Houston, and the film was *The Agony and the Ecstasy*, starring Charlton Heston as Michelangelo.

They even picked me up at our old five-room small farmhouse on Old Danbury Road. It always needed a paint job.

Although I was not scared by the highly elevated scaffolding with Michelangelo atop painting the Sistine Chapel, I was of Betty's father, Mr. O.V. McDaniel, because he was Angleton's School Superintendent. I wondered if he had seen my grades. Perhaps I could get them up to Cs, maybe even one or two as Bs. I doubted my A in athletics would be enough to impress. As with most fears in life, this was unfounded. Neither Betty nor her parents cared about what I drove or if our house needed painting.

Before I met Betty, I developed a celebrity crush on Janet Lennon while watching *The Lawrence Welk Show* in the 50s. "Wunnerful, Wunnerful! and Ah-One, Ah-Two!" And "Now here's the lovely Lennon Sisters," Welk would say. It was my Dad's fault for insisting we watched that show. Only rich folks owned two TVs, and I had no other choice.

My other celebrity crush in the '50s was Annette Funicello. She was among the most popular Mouseketeers in the original *Walt Disney Mickey Mouse Club*.

I never mentioned their names to my friends in elementary school; I didn't dare tell anyone for fear they would make fun of me. By age ten, I was over both of them.

Mr. O.V. McDaniel never gave me a reason to fear him. Still, I was as intimidated by him as I was when former President Lyndon Johnson was a surprise guest lecturer in Government 2320 a few years later at Southwest Texas State University. I dared not reach out to shake his hand. He later shook hands and signed autographs at the Commons Dining Hall on campus. I still did not approach him.

51

LBJ Teaching Government 2320 SWTSU
I was in another class upstairs.

Betty's parents influence me more with their gracious and classy lifestyle. They had a HiFi record console in their living room with a 78-rpm vinyl phonograph record on the turntable of Dean Martin often crooning.

Daddy had raised me on "rock 'n roll" stars like Hank Williams Sr and Ernest Tubb, although "Rock Stars" like Merle Haggard and Willie Nelson would become my favorites in college. And later, a student at Southwest Texas State named George Strait would top them all.

If you make it to heaven before me, don't you dare tell Daddy I once bought a complete set of Dean Martin's greatest hits from Time Life Music on TV?

Randy Willis and Betty McDaniel Valentine's Day 1966

Trust me when I sing *That's Amore.* you'd have to be higher than a Georgia Pine to make it through this verse with a straight face, "When the moon hits your eye like a big pizza pie." Taylor Swift needs to cut that song about her next beau.

The Beacon Theatre opened in Angleton at 201 E. Myrtle Street on February 16, 1968, with Steve McQueen in *The Sand Pebbles*. Within months, I'd be living on the campus of Southwest Texas State College, soon to be a University. I met Steve McQueen four years later near the SWTSU campus while he was filming *The Getaway*.

My fears faded as I became as sophisticated as a Hayseed Cowboy could be and "over-educated" as a Freshman college boy, to add insult to injury.

That is until one evening in Dallas in 1980. I was in the big city for a business trip, and as fate would have it, my friend from high school and college, Glen Hardwick, was also in town for advanced flight training at Love Field. We decided to see a new film entitled *The Shining*. It was like no movie I ever saw. It would be my last "picture show" of that type to watch.

I'd never read a Stephen King book. I practiced several of his writing suggestions today, including never using adverbs ending in "ly," and it's okay for emphasis to write a paragraph with one sentence. He proved that with a two-word paragraph in *The Shining*.

As writer Jack Torrance (Jack Nicholson) descends into madness, he seeks to kill his wife, Shelley Duvall, with an axe.

Like Audrey Hepburn, Shelley Duvall does not deserve this treatment. You will not find that on Google. It's my "unique" insight.

She locks herself in the bathroom of the haunted remote hotel in the Colorado mountains.

I understand a writer going crazy writing a book, but imitating Ed McMahon's introduction of Johnny Carson was clever, not crazy. It also is the scariest scene I've seen.

As Jack axes his way through the door, he sticks his smiling face through a hole in the door and exclaims,

"Here's Johnny."

Since then, I have preferred iconic lines like "Life is like a box of chocolate." You will never see Forrest Gump with an axe. Please hand me another Dr. Pepper Forrest. Are their bottle caps worth anything? If not, I'll start making t-shirts and bumper stickers.

Frankenstein Meets the Wolf Man

Wait Until Dark at the Lake Theater
in Lake Jackson, Texas.

Don Theater Alexander, Louisiana

The saddest scene in my life was those kids segregated in a balcony at the Don Theater. They entered through the 2nd door.

Lake Theater Lake Jackson, Texas

"I so earnestly believe that prayer can be helpful and guide you and protect you and inspire you. I mean, I'm in awe."
—*Horton Foote* Wharton, Texas

✫   ✫   ✫

CHAPTER 9
HURRICANE CARLA
GONE WITH THE WIND
ANGLETON, TEXAS 1960-1968

In 1960, we moved from 519 Coleman Street in Clute, Texas, to three miles East of Angleton, Texas, on Old Danbury Road (The corner of County Road 210 and County Road 212 today).

Our two-bedroom, tiny living room, kitchen, and one-bathroom framed home needed painting for the next eight years. My sister Marjorie, brother Buddy, and I shared one of the bedrooms and a small screen-in porch with a bed. Marjorie got the porch. It had a colossal exhaust window fan that made a distinctive noise. Later, I would have difficulty sleeping in college without that annoying clanging sound.

All three of us had separate tiny single beds. Two of the most incredible days of my life were when my brother and my sister moved out to get married. For the first time, I had a bedroom all by myself. I was in high cotton. We were not as rich as those in Angleton, who had brick houses with three bedrooms and a bath and a half. Some even had a carport. That was my mother's dream, anyhow.

✫   ✫   ✫

Two men who grew up 40 miles west of Angleton in the small community of Wharton would affect my life, although in very different ways.

Horton Foote received an Academy Award for his screenplay of the 1962 film *To Kill a Mockingbird*, adapted from the 1960 novel of the same name by Harper Lee.

Like Hurrance Carla in 1961, the movie *To Kill a Mockingbird*, a year later, left a lasting impression on me about my choices.

Dan Rather

Dan Rather grew up in Wharton, like Horton Foote. His grandmother   told him, "Dan, being in the middle of a hurricane is about as close as you will get to God." She had lived through the deadliest hurricane in the history of the US, the Galveston Hurricane of 1900, which killed more than 6,000 people.

Dan Rather, an unknown reporter at Houston's lowest-rated TV station, KHOU-TV, had an idea. Intrigued with hurricanes because of his grandmother's stories, Rather began to follow Hurricane Carla. He surmised it might hit Galveston.

He also suspected it might be a big story and wanted to cover the storm live from the National Weather Center in Galveston. He first had to convince his Program Director, who was initially against the idea—it had never been done and was risky.

Dan Rather had to convince the National Weather Center in Galveston to allow him and one cameraman to cover the storm live. They had a new radar system that had rarely been

59

used for weather. They, too, finally agreed. Rather knew both decisions must be made now because Carla was intensifying and headed their way.

Dan Rather, his KHOU-TV cameraman, began broadcasting from the National Weather Center in Galveston, showing the first radar image of a hurricane on TV. 1961 was the first year hurricanes were spotted on the TIROS-III satellite.

The radar image was mesmerizing but not relatable to the viewing audience. Dan Rather conceived the idea of overlaying a transparent map of Texas over the radar screen to show the audience the size of Hurricane Carla. The monster storm covered almost the entire Texas Gulf Coast. The KHOU staff back in Houston collectively said, "WOW," and so did the viewing public, and the public began to flee.

Convinced of the threat, more than 350,000 people evacuated from the area, the largest known evacuation to that date. Their actions saved hundreds of lives, maybe more.

New York and national stations broadcast live coverage of Carla. America was glued to their TV sets as Carla grew 400 miles wide, with the eye 50 miles across and with 150 plus mph wind. Carla would grow even more expansive and reach a maximum sustained wind speed of around 170 mph.

Dan Rather and Weather Bureau radar expert Vaughn Rockney, brought in from Washington, kept the audience updated for three days on Carla's movement.

Two years later, Dan Rather would be in Dallas on November 22, 1963, near Dealey Plaza, thirty yards from the soon-to-be infamous grassy knoll. This story would be more significant than Carla in Texas and the world.

Our farmhouse on Old Danbury Road was along the Coastal Bend at an elevation of 15 feet with high humidity and billions of mosquitos when the winds died. We were only 18 miles from the Gulf of Mexico as the crow flies.

That 15 feet and 18 miles barely saved our home from Hurricane Carla in September 1961. Another "decision" would save our lives.

We had fled to our old homeplace in Longleaf, Louisiana, in Central Louisiana, to avoid the first named Hurricane of 1957, Audrey. The Category 3 hurricane killed 416 people due primarily to the 12-foot storm surge that reached 20 miles inland.

Surely, Hurricane Carla would not be that strong. Audrey was one of the deadliest hurricanes in US history.

Carla moved northwest and strengthened to a sizeable major hurricane over the Gulf of Mexico on the evening of September 7. The winds increased to around 175 mph early on September 11, making Carla a Category 5 hurricane.

"We need to leave," Mother said.

"We fled Hurricane Audrey four years ago, and it followed us to Louisiana. We are staying put," Daddy replied.

Within a couple of hours, two Brazoria County Sheriff's Deputies arrived. I stood close to Daddy on the front porch and overheard one deputy say, "Mr Willis, the High Sheriff, said to tell you to leave now." The deputy added; the Sheriff also said to tell you, sir, "That's not a suggestion."

61

Daddy turned red and loaded Mother, me, and my sister Marjorie into our Rambler Station Wagon. We made it as far as a rice field north of Egypt, Texas. That was the longest 60-mile drive of my life. Elvis never shook like that Rambler did that night. Daddy was right: Carla followed us, but west this time. But, the elevation was over 100 feet higher than our home on Old Danbury Road.

Robert Dunn

Another boy, 15-year-old Angleton High School student Robert Dunn, was less fortunate. He lost 11 family members in the monstrous storm surge on Bastrop Bayou south of Angleton that night. In a later interview, he was asked, "Why did you all stay?"

"My Dad said we made it through Hurricane Audrey, and we're staying."

On the 40th Anniversary of Robert Dunn's loss, September 11, 2001, another tragedy would occur, but this time at the Twin Towers in lower Manhattan. Its elevation was not an advantage.

Robert Dunn died on September 12, 1968, in 106th General Hospital, Yokohama, Japan, of burns received when a flash fire swept through powder stores he was helping to demolish in South Vietnam. He died seven years and one day after the death of his family in Hurricane Carla. My friend Glen Hardwick said when we visited Robert's grave, it might have been on the same day, with the many time zone changes.

Robert Dunn is buried next to his family in the Angleton Cemetery. I revisited his grave the last time I laid a flower on my two brothers' graves, also buried in the Angleton Cemetery.

Brownie Rhodes

Since then, I've never had to be warned twice to flee a hurricane. We made it another 30 miles to the Columbus, Texas Courthouse the following day. We couldn't stay there; the roof had blown off. We slept on the gym floor under an arched top that covered the Columbus High School gym. The Red Cross fed us.

The next day, we decided to take our box lunches, get out of that stifling gym, and plan our next step. We headed north on the old Highway 71 and stopped at a roadside park north of the Colorado River. Sitting at a concrete park table was a man that Daddy knew. He was distraught and exhausted. His name was Brownie Rhodes.

I don't recall the conversation except when Mr. Rhodes told of his cows and horses climbing atop the irrigation canal levees to escape the rising water only to be greeted by hundreds of agitated water moccasins and rattlesnakes.

Suddenly, our problems seemed minor. That image has never left me. Mr. Rhodes had a truck filled with everything from furniture to monkeys. He reminded me of John Steinbeck's Tom Joad that day, played by Henry Fonda in *The Grapes of Wrath*. Although I learned when we returned home and toured the damages caused by Carla, including Mr. Rhodes's home from the road, he was far from poor, although he may have felt that way after Hurricane Carla.

On November 2, 2002, *The Brazosport Facts* said of the then 94-year-old rancher, "Lawson Brownie Rhodes was raising cattle in Brazoria County before Dow Chemical or Lake Jackson were a part of the landscape. Rhodes, who lives in Oyster Creek, began with 74 head of cattle in 1938 and built it into a successful family business that spans three

63

generations. The business now has more than 800 head of cattle across 30,000 acres of land.

"He [Mr. Rhodes] said the worst storm he endured was Hurricane Carla in 1961. The hurricane killed 235 of his cattle and nearly destroyed his home. He found one of his cows inside a home in Richwood and some other cattle as far north as Alvin."

Once we returned home, we discovered our farmhouse, sitting on its two-foot-high blocks, escaped the rising water by two inches. Our butane tank had floated off, but our few cows and horses were safe in knee-deep water. They stayed out of our barn, I'm sure, because of the snakes. Horses are intelligent.

Carla pushed a storm surge of 22 feet above sea level at the head of Lavaca Bay in Port Lavaca—the highest storm surge in Texas history.

Hurricane Carla was the most intense hurricane to hit Texas in the 20th century. I never knew if the Good Lord sent those deputies or if one of His Angels named Mama did.

KHOU-TV Houston moved its cameras to the U. S. Weather Bureau's Galveston headquarters where for more than three days Weather Bureau radar expert Vaughn Rockney (l) and Dan Rather, KHOU-TV's news director, briefed viewers on the movements of Hurricane Carla.

Robert Dunn, the only survivor of a family of 12 in Hurricane Carla, south of Angleton, Texas, is greeted by Texas Governor Price Daniel and Vice President Lyndon Johnson in Freeport, Texas.

'They were holding hands ...and then they were gone'

"I begged Daddy to go," Dunn told a Houston Chronicle reporter right after the storm, "but he wouldn't leave. He said he'd been in storms before. So I stayed, too."

Rising water forced the family into the attic, where they spent a fearful day and night as the storm pounded the house.

"We only had a loaf of bread," Robert Dunn told a reporter. "My share was two slices. Two younger children were crying from hunger, so I divided my share. I didn't feel hungry anyway," he added.

"Then a big wave came," he said. "All of us started for the roof. I got up there. Two children tried to grab my hand, but something seemed to pull them away from me.

"I saw the water come up to my little brothers' necks, and I reached down my hand to them, but the waves went right out over them, and Mother and Daddy were holding hands, and Mother was crying, and then they were gone," he sobbed.

My maternal grandmother, Nina Ruth Hanks Lawson, is at our home on Old Danbury Road. Our home escaped the rising water from Hurricane Carla by two inches. My friend Bill Adam's barn, a mile and a half closer to the Gulf of Mexico, had six feet of water. As the crow flies, our 40-acre farm was 18 miles from the Gulf of Mexico.

Grandma started singing the old gospel tune on our front porch, *Shall We Gather at the River*. We almost did for the last time.

★ ★ ★

CHAPTER 10
OLD DANBURY ROAD
ANGLETON, TEXAS 1960-1968

O ur Old Danbury Road home included 40 acres, a barn, and chicken coops. The rent was $40 monthly in 1960 but rose to $50 by the mid-60s. I wondered what we must sacrifice to make up the $10. I lived there until a month after my high school graduation in May 1968.

As a boy growing up on Old Danbury Road, I mostly saw rice fields and Ed Bieri's San Gertrudis cattle across Old Danbury Road. Our window screens would be caked with mosquitos as our giant window fan seemed to glue them to the screens at night.

Flocks of snow geese would arrive on the Texas Coast to winter in fallow fields and marshlands. The land surrounding our farmhouse would appear solid white. I was happy in a farm boy's paradise.

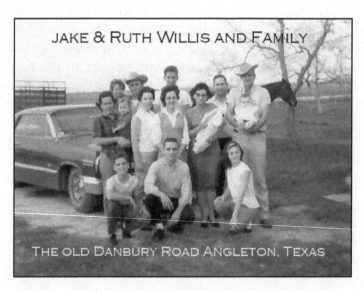

JAKE & RUTH WILLIS AND FAMILY

THE OLD DANBURY ROAD ANGLETON, TEXAS

Brazos River Bottomland

Between ages 10 and 14, we worked cows every weekend on the Brazos River bottomland. Daddy and Red Amos from Angleton were partners. They leased two large pastures. One was on the banks of the Brazos, and the other was on FM 521 north of Anchor.

In those days, getting to our Brazos River bottomland wasn't easy. After driving to Anchor, Texas, we went west on County Road 30, past Holiday Lakes, and a couple miles on horseback to the area near today's Brazos River County Park on the Brazos River. There was only one hitch: we had to swim our saddle horses through a vast slough. After that, it was a heavy forest.

This land inspired two stories in my novels, *Three Winds Blowing* and *Texas Wind*. The first is when Daddy and his quarter horse gelding named Joe almost drowned swimming the slough. As a water moccasin approached old Joe, he went berserk and ended up on top of Daddy as he got entangled in his rope.

Mama and I were concerned when it got dark; you did not dare ride a horse through that country after sunset. We both breathed a sigh of relief two hours later as Daddy climbed out of his pickup, still soaking wet after the long drive home. "Can you unsaddle Joe and feed him, son? We will unhitch the trailer in the morning," Daddy said.

I'm unsure who was more worn out, Old Joe or Daddy. When I got Joe to our barn, I could barely slide the heavy, wet saddle, rope, saddle bags, and Daddy's 30-30 Winchester off Old Joe's back. Yes, the gun was still in the saddle's rifle sheath—something Daddy had never done before after working cows.

69

I cried and thanked the Good Lord for both of their safe return. Daddy never swam Old Joe across that slough alone again. I was only 12, but I remember it like it was yesterday. Before that night, I rarely prayed for Daddy, for he seemed invincible. That changed that night as I realized he wasn't bulletproof. Those prayers would soon be needed again.

☆   ☆   ☆

Months passed when Daddy, my brother Jerry, and I would have an adventure in the water almost as dangerous but way more exciting. I have told this story many times to my children and grandchildren.

As we drove our cattle to a makeshift set of cattle pens near the banks of the swollen Brazos River, one of the calves decided he could swim the swirling waters. As Jerry rode down the steep embankment to rescue the calf, Daddy yelled, "Jerry, don't, you and your horse will both drown."

Then Daddy turned and called to his Catahoula Leopard Dog, "Bob, catch him." Bob swam to the middle of the swift Brazos and grabbed the calf's ear in his mouth. After the calf turned towards us, Bob's mouth was clamped to the calf's tail. They both arrived safely—almost 200 feet downriver. Daddy dismounted, called Bob, petted, and praised him for a well-done job.

Bob was the most intelligent dog I ever knew, including Jack. Daddy purchased him in Louisiana and trained him in Texas. My God, I love the cowboy way of life.

Jack and Bob would later lose an eye near our farmhouse on Old Danbury Road, grabbing hold of a horse and later mule's tail with their teeth.

But they were still more enthusiastic about their work with one eye than most cowboys were with two, a new 4-wheel drive Chevy pickup and a pretty girl sitting close to them in a tight pair of Wranglers tucked in Lucchese Boots.

My brother Jerry Duke on Majestic

After riding on a trail ride all day, Jerry died near Shiner, Texas. He was pronounced dead at the Yoakum Community Hospital. Jerry was the type of person that everyone liked.

My brother Jerry's funeral with both flags he loved flying above his casket in a mule-drawn wagon (aka as a pickup). No team could pull that many friends.

We will ride together again. Jerry may even have a better horse than me, as he always did when we were boys. Well, that's okay.

CHAPTER 11
RED AMOS
ANGLETON, TEXAS 1964-1968

Red Amos was one of the best men I ever knew. He was a devout elder at the Angleton Church of Christ. Daddy was a backslidden Southern Baptist. They were partners and a perfect match because of two words: trust and respect.

Their theological discussions would go like this:" "Jake, we can't buy a Hereford bull; those whiteface cattle are prone to getting pinkeye."

"Well, Red, how about we buy one of Ed Bieri's San Gertrudis bulls?"

"Do you have any idea what they cost?" Red replied.

"Well then, let's buy another Brahman bull and stick to what we know, crossbreeding," Daddy said. They both knew Brahmans could thrive in the South Texas heat and insects.

That was church, except on Sundays, because Red Amos did not work on Sundays. They were exact opposites, but it worked because they both were men of high integrity and trusted each other. They remained close friends to the end of their lives. There is a verse in Isaiah in the Book they practiced, although they never quoted it, "Come now, and let us reason together."

Chapter 12
The Salt Grass Cattle Company
1963-1966

Our cow punching would triple in '63. I was 13 and riding anything with four legs, including Jersey Milk Cows with Billy Adams and Earl Goodrum. Billy's Dad, JW Adams, had a set of cattle pens with bucking shoots. Earl's Dad, Dude Goodrum, a cowboy's cowboy, was JW Adams's foreman. I watched a wedding on horseback in that arena once. The preacher, groom, and bride were all on horses.

It was fun until a cow threw me and stepped on my ankle. I rode my horse a mile and a half home at a trot and used my pocket knife to cut off my left boot because of the swelling. When I attempted to show Daddy, he didn't look up from his Zane Grey or Louis L'Amour Western novel. That was his way of saying, "Get over it."

I reckoned when you just read Wild Bill Hickok killed a dozen outlaws, or was it 200, nothing short of death deserved an acknowledgment. I felt I had to get tough or die, and sometimes, I felt dying would have been easier.

In 1963, several ranchers formed the Salt Grass Cattle Company in the Saltgrass Country of Brazoria County and owned a feed and saddle store on the left side of Highway 35, a couple of miles from Angleton towards Alvin. The Registered Agent was JW Adams, founded on May 20, 1963.

The Salt Grass Cattle Company leased much of its land from Jack Phillips, a local rancher, although all the ranchers owned or leased their separate cattle spreads. Salt Grass was two words, like the trail ride, not the steakhouse for those taking notes.

74

Daddy was friends with JW Adams, Dude Goodrum, Babe Scott, Red Bennett, and Melvin Staples. Mr. Staples lived near our pasture on FM 521 north of Anchor, Texas.

Daddy's other partner in the cow business, Red Amos, was never involved with the Salt Grass Cattle Company; he was a Church of Christ Elder in Angleton and never missed church, much less be seen near a can of Lone Star Beer.

JW Adams was our closest neighbor (a mere mile and a half) from our farmhouse on Old Danbury Road. Babe Scott's barns were towards the Angleton Fairgrounds. And Red Bennett was from Danbury. When you live in the country, those folks are called close neighbors.

They all were involved with The Salt Grass Cattle Company. I felt as if I was watching the epic Western *Giant*. Mr. Adam would have been Bick Benedick.

But I was more fascinated by Jett Rick in *Giant*. The rags-to-riches life story of the Texas wildcatter oil tycoon Glenn McCarthy inspired the character Jett Rink.

In Brazoria County (1946), McCarthy drilled the highest-pressure gas well in Texas—the world then.

Bryan Burrough recounts McCarthy's epic rise and fall in his book *The Big Rich: The Rise and Fall of the Greatest Texas Oil Fortunes*. Burrough wrote Glenn McCarthy's most tremendous success as an oilman came in areas he knew, such as "the swamplands and buggy moors south and east of

75

Houston." Among these were Angleton and Chocolate Bayou.

I became interested in McCarthy in college when I dated a girl from West Columbia who worked for him. She and I are still friends. She shared a few stories about McCarthy. I was mesmerized.

None of the characters in *Giant* were like any of us, but I dreamed as a 13-year-old boy. In my novel *Texas Wind*, Ken Willis (my actual great-uncle) was inspired by Glenn McCarthy.

Jake Willis & Randy Willis

Daddy and me in The Salt Grass Country
Brazoria County near Danbury, Texas

☆   ☆   ☆

CHAPTER 13
SUNDAY MORNING COMING DOWN

The men of the Salt Grass Cattle Company often met after a long, hard day at the Roundup on IH 35 (Mulberry Street). It was on the left side of 35 towards Alvin, a few hundred yards past Cedar Street. It had three rooms: a bar area, a small room with a pool table, and a larger room with a dance floor with a jukebox with lots of Hank Williams and Lefty Frizzell playing. It was the Salt Grass Cattle Company's unofficial office.

Lonestar Beer was a quarter. No one drank those "foreign" beers like Budweiser. There were always six to eight men at the table. The wives and children sometimes came because it was a place where your family felt comfortable. I hung out in the pool room with my friends.

Mary and Adolph Zapalac, the owners, kept a keen eye on the table, looking for a nod to bring another round. No one bought a single beer unless they arrived late. It was always a round—no need to overwork Mary and Adolph, although they always seemed to be standing.

After one or two or three rounds, everyone went home. No one was there to get drunk, chase women, or get into fights like the movies showed.

Our home phone was a party line with six or more other homes who could and did listen to our conversations. Many of the phones in the country had party lines. We didn't have to go through a switchboard operator like Andy Griffith did with Sarah, but if you wanted to spread a rumor, a party line was as good as Facebook is today.

78

The Roundup was an excellent place to discuss business without Brazoria County knowing the Salt Grass Cattle Company's plans.

The Roundup was a way to privately send a text or an e-mail many decades before they were invented, but my Mama disapproved because of the beer. Daddy promised her when they married in 1948 that he'd never take another drink of alcohol.

The Round Up today. Angleton, Texas

Mother saw what I never witnessed until later: Daddy was not a "good drunk." Mama grew up next door to Daddy on Willis Gunter Road near Longleaf, Louisiana. She was best friends with his mother, Lillie.

She knew that Daddy's father, my namesake, Randall Lee "Rand" Willis, drank a mason jar of moonshine daily down on the banks of Barber Creek near Longleaf, Louisiana, away from Grandma's disapproving eyes. Grandpa died at age 54. Mama and Grandma never allowed a can of beer in their homes, which Daddy respected. But Mama did not want the Roundup to become Daddy's Barber Creek.

✯   ✯   ✯

In a strange dichotomy, mother always spiked her fruitcakes with some rum. "It's no different from using cooking sherry; it provides moisture and helps preserve the cake," she said.

We tried to find where she hid the rum during the holidays but never could, but I did have more than one slice, maybe several.

My grandmother Lillie's definition of a mortal sin was sterner. She wouldn't use the home remedy for teething fussy babies, a dash of whiskey and honey rubbed on their gums. Watching her husband and my Grandpa, Randall Lee "Rand" Willis, die slowly over a decade at age 54 from alcoholism will give you an attitude.

Grandpa's footstone from his grave blocked us (us as in my cousins) from mowing around his headstone, so my first cousin Donnie Willis moved the stone from the Graham Cemetery near Forest Hill, Louisiana, to his home in Fenton, Louisiana, many years ago.

Donnie's brother and my first cousin Ray Willis told him I should have our Grandpa's footstone since he was my namesake. Ray took it to his home in Lindale, Texas. A couple of months ago, he called me and said he had a meeting in Austin and would drive it to my home in the Texas Hill Country if I wanted the stone.

The journey from Fenton to the Texas Hill Country reminded me of Captain Call hauling Captain Augustus "Gus" McCrae's body in the movie *Lonesome Dove*, but I was honored to have it.

You remember, after a long, dangerous journey from Montana or one of those icebergs, Captain Call buries Gus by a spring in an orchard near San Antonio, where he used to picnic with Clara.

Sorry, Grandpa, I'm not planting an orchard. But I may have your great-great-grandson Corbin plant one this Spring.

My grandson Corbin placed the stone in my circle drive. Grandpa and I talk daily, but never about moonshine. There's no need. I got the point. At least it wasn't from an arrow like Gus.

Captain Call said, "Anything gets boring if you talk about it enough, even death." Let us move on.

Daddy's first drink in 15 years was not the only issue. Working cows on the Lord's Day was, too. Mama knew telling Daddy not to work on Sundays was wishful thinking since he ran a few muley-headed cows and worked shiftwork at Dow Chemical, but what about the low-hanging fruit, me?

Mama told Daddy, "Randy needs to be in church." My letter of transfer (which showed I was a baptized member in good standing since age eight) had already been mailed from Temple Baptist in Clute to Second Baptist in Angleton weeks before.

Our brand, Bar-D-K, has been our family
since 1866, the end of the Civil War.

Mother, Ruth Willis, headed to
Temple Baptist in Clute, Texas. 1956

Now, Daddy could argue like a Philadelphia lawyer, so he posed a question to Mother that he already knew the answer to based on his deductive reasoning. "Let's let Randy decide." I loved horses, working cows, the cowboy way of life, and John Wayne; therefore, the case was settled. At least, that's what Daddy thought.

I asked for an hour to decide. Let's see, I get up at 5:30 on Sunday mornings or at 8:00. Saddle a half dozen horses, or dust off my Bible. A couple hours at church or eight to ten in the pastures. A 100 degrees in the salt grass country or 72 degrees in the church: a billion mosquitoes or none.

I still could not decide until I remembered there were no rattlesnakes at church; at least none were allowed to bite you. I became a self-serving, semi-devoted, and self-righteous

83

believer. I never encountered that type of "snake" at Temple Baptist in Clute or Second Baptist in Angleton, but I later would.

All this was because my mother took a stand on Lonestar Beer and where I needed to be on Sundays, hopefully, you wonder. Well, not all of it; there was and is Another.

My friend, Glen Hardwick, told me once, "You are acting like Jake Willis ." The question is always, which of my parents influenced me more on a given day? The answer is both, and that's where the overused phrase comes into play, "It's complicated." In other words, I'm no door prize. Thank the Good Lord, though; He is not the author of confusion.

A few truths I've learned along the way are many people have just enough religion to inoculate them from knowing Jesus. And we all fall short of the Glory of God. And the more I study the Book, the more I realize how little I know Him.

Josh Willis, Bro. J.B. Young, and Aaron Willis.

Baby Shower at Mima's Restaurant in Wimberley,
Texas, for Arron and Alana Willis's
Future Baby Baylee Willis.

My sons Josh and Aaron Willis with Bro. JB Young.

I know; once again, I am getting ahead of my story.
Where was I? I believe it was Brazoria County in the
1960s.

☆   ☆   ☆

85

CHAPTER 14
THE BRAZORIA NATIONAL WILDLIFE REFUGE

The Brazoria National Wildlife Refuge was established during my junior year in high school in 1966. It began with 6,398 acres, half bought from rancher Jack Phillips. It was on this same land that we worked cows on almost every weekend between 1963 and 1966.

The Salt Grass Cattle Company's lease from Mr. Phillips covered from south of FM 2004 and east of County Road 208 (Peltier Road) to County Road 227 (Hoskins Mound Road). My education of how to be a cowman (there was no boy in this training) advanced to graduate school as a teenager.

The school was named the Salt Grass Cattle Company. Earl Goodrum, Pruitt Scott, Billy Adams, Bubba Bennett, my brother Jerry, me, and others would learn from our fathers, Dude Goodrum, Babe Scott, JW Adams, Red Bennett, and Jake Willis. The lessons included roping, riding, castrating, drenching, and vaccinating cattle while avoiding getting killed.

"If you get killed, your mama is going to be upset with me," Daddy would often tell me. Ole Cowboys, like ole football coaches, had a way of encouraging you.

But it was all worth it because calf fries would later be ready at the cattle pens for lunch prepared by the wives. I always brought a sandwich or two in my saddlebags because I was taught not to be greedy. That reminds me of George Strait's song *Ocean Front Property*.

Julian "Jake" Willis

☆   ☆   ☆

Every once in a while, in The Texas Hill Country where I now reside, I can hear the honking sound of the Canadian geese as they fly south. They use that sound to coordinate their shifts within their V-formation. It reminds me that kids growing up in Brazoria County today will hear and see 100,000 geese and other species as I did as a boy. That honking sound always makes me smile.

In 1986, the Brazoria National Wildlife Refuge expanded by managing the Slop Bowl addition, which it acquired from the Nature Conservancy. That brought back memories, too, but not nearly as good as the Salt Grass Cattle Company.

The first time I hunted ducks was in the Slop Bowl. It was in the early 60s when Daddy joined the Muldoon Hunting and Fishing Club. I remember a vast hunting lodge near Otter Slough and a long row of Model T's—duck blinds on the banks and in the middle of a freshwater lake.

Ford Model A's and T's had been used in the Slop Bowl for decades. Ford Motor Company promoted the Model T's reliability by entering two cars in the 1909 Transcontinental Race from New York to Seattle over the rough country when roads were nearly nonexistent. I have often wondered what became of them.

What I remember most was the mud, rattlesnakes, and mosquitoes. Did I say more mud than you can imagine? I have never experienced anything like it since, nor do I wish to again.

When Al Bisbey hunted there in the 1960s, he remembered, "You had to walk backward because of the mosquitoes. That was the only way you could breathe."

For a century, the Slop Bowl overwhelmed hunters, cattle, and mule-drawn wagons. Frank Brazill drove a Model A Ford to the Slop Bowl to build duck blinds. When he didn't return, Brownie Rhodes found him stranded. Mr. Rhodes could barely recognize him after the mosquitoes had their way. He was trapped in the mud and surrounded by rattlesnakes in his Model A Ford.

A former Angleton mayor named Neal Giesecke found himself lost in the Slop Bowl and wandered for so long, looking for help, that he eventually was hospitalized.

Another time, Mr. Rhodes drove cows through the marsh and killed at least 51 rattlesnakes. Teams of mules and cows would sink in the mud and suffocate.

Then why did you hunt there, Randy? You may be wondering by now. Jack Taylor said it best, "This gigantic pit of filth was known far and wide for having the best duck hunting to be found anywhere along the Texas Gulf Coast."

RK Sawyer's *A Hundred Years* of *Texas Waterfowl Hunting: The Decoys, Guides, Clubs, and Places, 1870s to 1970s,* has an excellent chapter (nine) on Brazoria County.

Daddy, my brothers, and I started hunting deer and turkey in the Texas Hill Country during college. I never had a problem hunting for the next half-century—at least when I compared it to Brazoria County's Slop Bowl. But then again, I would like to see 10,000 Canadian geese take flight at least one more time. Well, maybe two or three with my grandchildren.

What's a tiny bit of wet dirt, a couple of mosquitoes, and a few snakes to a rugged ole hayseed cowboy like me? Then I woke up, turned the air conditioner down, and tuned into the Nature Channel, or was that the RFID channel? Can someone bring me a cup of coffee and maybe a hot biscuit with butter?

As a ten-year-old boy, I fancied myself a mighty hunter with my 410 shotgun. I first shot it in the Slop Bowl.

But when that came to an end, I sought other hunting grounds. I had strict instructions from Daddy not to fire my gun toward other people's property. "This is not the Slop Bowl," he said.

One day, a massive goose of a different color from the Canadian geese came strutting down Old Danbury Road like a Peacock. I was sure his color was a freak thing. Indeed, he was fair game. We soon had roasted goose for supper.

A day or two later, Mr. Ed Bieri dropped by our old farmhouse and asked me if I had seen his prized show goose by chance. Indeed, I thought this was a coincidence, so I said, "No, sir." That was the last goose I saw strutting down Old Danbury Road.

Due to the recent decline in the goose population, I switched to hunting Bobwhite Quail. I reckoned no one showed them at the Brazoria County Fair. I even learned their whistling call. I can still do it, but not as loud. After I did the Bobwhite call for my Grandson Corbin, I asked him how it sounded. He replied, "How did what sound?" Now I know how Roger Dangerfield felt.

Daddy once got mad at me for taking the keys out of one of our pickups. "What if someone breaks down on these backroads and needs to borrow it?" I never took them out again. I didn't have to worry about our house keys, for we never owned any.

We never caught a fish or killed an animal we or someone else did not eat. I ate deer, squirrel, rabbit, quail, and duck and once tasted cow tongue at Daddy's insistence. I never ate Eggs' n' brains (a breakfast meal consisting of pork brains and scrambled eggs), but Daddy did. My tastes are far less exotic today than Daddy or my grandson Corbin Willis, who will even eat liver. Corbin reminds me of Daddy.

When Daddy bought "Joe," he was a stallion and would rear up on his hind legs and fall backward on top of any rider. No one would dare buy him until that day.

Daddy "corrected" both of those issues. He began by turning this stud into a gelding. Although he never became a "kid horse," I rode him working cows at age 12 and once roped another horse named Dixie on him in a narrow holding pen in the corner of our pasture. I could not catch the 900-pound mare with feed. When Dixie hit the rope's end, Joe and I stood proud.

That lasted two seconds after she whipped around like the Nyon rope was a rubber band, and it was. Then she headed straight past us in the very narrow opening with twice the distance to build up speed. I had but one thought in my mind, "Oh no!"

Before I could turn Joe, Dixie hit the rope's end again. I learned how well a Buck Steiner saddle and Joe were built. I also decided my horse roping days were over when I realized my arm almost got tangled in the rope. A good horse and saddle can save your life, but you also need common sense.

91

My niece Patricia Duke, brother Jerry Duke, and me, Randy Willis (holding the reins on Joe). I was ten years old. The Old Danbury Road, Angleton, Texas, 1960.

Joe was part of the family. He was as stout as a John Deere tractor in low gear.

"You know horses are smarter than people. You never heard of a horse going broke betting on people." — Will Rogers

☆   ☆   ☆

CHAPTER 15
$10 HORSES & $40 SADDLES

B etween 1960 and 1968, it seemed all we did was work cows.

And break horses and mules in preparation for the Brazoria County Trailride. Daddy was Trailboss for nine years, so saddle up, take a deep seat, and keep your mind in the middle as 2,000 riders, horses, mules, wagons, and buggies ride for four days.

Jake Willis (left) Trailboss, Brazoria County Trailride

And visit old friends around a campfire before dancing till midnight. Wake the following day at sunrise, listening to

93

Eddy Arnold's *Cattle Call* from the Lone Star Beer Sound Truck.

JAKE WILLIS
BRAZORIA COUNTY
TRAIL RIDE

After four days, finish by riding in the Brazoria County Parade to kick off the largest county fair in Texas, which means the world, The Brazoria County Fair and Rodeo.

Our interest in cattle, horses, and mules overlapped from Louisiana to Texas during those years.

The bad news is we didn't make much money in the beef cow-calf business. The good news is that it wasn't nearly as bad as the horse business. At least our saddles remained "steady."

It didn't matter if feeder steers and heifers were selling high or low; we always rode the best saddles made in Texas, which meant the world. Saddles often cost more than a horse. But, then again, a good saddle could last much longer than a good horse, and it didn't eat, kick, bite, and try to commit suicide.

My Dad bought me a Buck Steiner saddle from Capitol Saddlery in Austin in the early '60s. I still own it, mounted on a stand in my office. The saddle had big, supportive swells for breaking horses. I soon needed those swells, although the first horse I broke almost broke me. After being thrown three times, Daddy said, "Let me have 'em." That was the last time that horse ever bucked. I was only 12; it would not be the last time a horse threw me.

By the time I reached 40, I had been to an emergency room thrice—all three times because of a horse. The first was when a mare turned her back on me faster than I moved. She almost kicked me in the head, but I reacted by lifting my right forearm. I still have a knot on it. They x-ray it. My arm was not broken, and they gave me a shot of Demerol. Daddy had taught me to be careful of horses when they were around new and strange horses. But she was alone. I found out she was in heat when she kicked me.

Horses may be aggressive around other horses feeding, and if a mare is in heat, she may see you as a potential mate and threaten you to stay away by biting and kicking. A horse may hurt you when other times they are as gentle as a "Kid Horse."

Saddles L to R: Frank Vela, Billy Cook, Buck Steiner
Saddles. My Office at my Texas Hill Country Home

No one told me the Buck Steiner saddle (far right, 14")
would get smaller over the years. At least, that's my story. I
ride a Billy Cook saddle today (center, 17"). His saddles were
meticulously hand-tooled. He was one of the best saddle
makers in Texas. In 1953, a young Billy Cook opened his
saddle shop in Greenville, Texas.

My Billy Cook saddle's seat is "slightly" more extensive
than my Buck Steiner one, a mere three inches. If that seat
shrinks, I will ride in a wagon, my GMC pickup, walk, or,
God forbid, go on a diet.

My Dad's saddle was made by Frank Vela (far left, 16")
in Floresville, Texas. Frank Vela made saddles with a
reputation for quality that spread throughout Texas and
beyond until he died in 1959. Vela saddles were in demand
by ranchers, cowboys, rodeo performers, and movie stars.
They are collector's items today.

L to R: Tommy Shane Steiner, Bobby Steiner, Sid Steiner, and Randy Willis.

I've been friends with the Steiners for many decades, including Bobby Steiner's Dad, Tommy Steiner, and his Grandfather, Buck Steiner. I have not met Sid's son, Rocker Steiner, but I have seen him on TV. Rocker and his sister Steely are the next in the Steiner family going back five generations in the rodeo. They are gracious, polite, and kind hearted folks. I'm honored to call them friends.

I decided two years ago to have Daddy's saddle made safe by Slade Paradeaux of Slade Saddle Shop in Luling. Slade worked for Frank Vela in Uvalde. He did an incredible job inspecting, repairing, and replacing everything needed. He did the same for my Billy Cook and Buck Steiner saddles.

My next hospital visit began on a frigid morning near Weimar, Texas, on the Texas Trail Ride to San Antonio. My Dad was an officer in that association for years. The ride initially began at Altair and later at Hallettsville. But, if I can recall, this morning near Weimar was only one of the few times we started there.

JOSH WILLIS & RANDY WILLIS

I'm riding my all-time favorite AQHA quarter horse mare "Spring." Born on the first day of Spring, she was out of the King Ranch's famous cutting horse, Mr. San Peppy. She could run like a deer and turn on a dime. My son Josh is riding "Big Boy"—so to speak—a quarter (of a) horse.

I saddled Spring once on a trail ride near Weimer, Texas, at sunrise. She bowed up and began to cop an attitude when I cinched my saddle. She had never done that before. As I climbed on, she began to buck. Somehow, she ended up on top of me.

I loaded her back into my trailer and drove 82 miles to San Marcos to the hospital. When I arrived, my left ankle was so swollen they had to cut my left boot off. Again, no broken bones. I've been fortunate; those were my two worst injuries in seven decades. That was the only time she ever bucked. I paid closer attention to the weather after that. Anything that causes a horse pain can be a problem. And it was colder than a politician's heart.

Have you ever met a person who is impossible to dislike? The kind of person that would give you their shirt off their back day or night.

Well, that was my brother Jerry. But I'm not going to talk about that. I prefer to talk about a night when he was not very nice.

My brother Jerry, our Dad Jake Willis, and I had ridden 25 miles on the first day of the Texas Trail Ride from Weimer to Hallettsville, Texas.

That night at the Hallettsville VFW, we camped. All three of us were hungry for the annual BBQ. There was a long line in the VFW Hall.

Jerry said something to my Dad that I could not hear. They walked to the front of the line and started a conversation with a trail rider who was as big as a defensive lineman for the Dallas Cowboys. I figured they were all friends until the cowboy started staring me down.

I knew I best investigate and walked up to the three of them just as Jerry said, "Yeah, mister, we don't know who he is, but he's been bragging he can whip your ass."

I responded, "Sir, this is my Dad and brother."

They both replied, "We don't know him."

The guy figured it out, looked at me, and smiled, "I'm not a fighter; I'm a lover."

I said as I looked up, "Thank you, Jesus."

Jerry and Daddy are both riding herd in Heaven now. I pray the angels to keep an eye on them in the BBQ line. I'll join them soon.

Jerry Duke, my brother, me, and my Dad, Jake Willis. Between Hallettsville and Shiner, headed to San Antonio.

One of the most awful things I see today is people advertising "Kid Horses" as safe as a lamb, bomb-proof. They show photos of small children riding them. Some are, and some are not gentle enough for a child. Be careful; they are not pet rabbits. Always err on the side of caution, especially with kids.

A half Shetland was the best we ever owned; my three sons named him "Big Boy." He was part of our family. I never bought another horse that short because they could hit the rider if another horse kicked at them.

Randy Willis on "Spring." And Aaron Willis is riding "Big Boy." Wimberley, Texas 4th of July Parade Aaron won 1st Place Best Horse & Rider! That was a big deal for both of us. The following year, Josh won.

Let me climb down from my soapbox.

Aaron Willis at our home in Wimberley, Texas.

JOSH, ADAM, RANDY & AARON WILLIS

Josh Willis 🐴 Adam Willis 🐴 Randy Willis 🐴 Aaron Willis

Josh Willis, Adam Willis, Randy Willis,
and Aaron Willis

Between Hallettsville and Shiner, headed to the San Antonio Rodeo. And Daddy's matching lineback dun mules Pete and Re-Pete. They were brothers like my three sons but not as stubborn.

☆　　☆　　☆

103

CHAPTER 16
BILLY ADAMS

Entertainment on Old Danbury Road included watching JK West crop dust in the surrounding fields.

Mr. West was taught how to fly by his father when he was only 16. Two years later, he joined The United States Army Air Corps (Airforce today) after the attack on Pearl Harbor by the Japanese in 1941. He was a friend of my Dad.

After World War II, West owned the M&M Airport at Bailes Field. Before buying them out, Mr. West flew for M&M as a crop-dusting pilot. That was back in the 50s. M&M was located on the Old Danbury Road between our home and Angleton. It is known as Bailes Airport today.

One of Mr. West's pilots almost pulled up too late as he approached an electrical line on telephone poles near our home. On the next pass, he flew underneath the electrical powerline. And then he did it again. I felt as if I was watching a stunt pilot. Nevertheless, I decided I would never make it as a pilot.

☆   ☆   ☆

We were in the middle of nowhere. My closest neighbor was a mile and a half down the dusty Marine Shell Road (County Road 212 today). His name was Billy Adams. We become best friends.

We both loved horses, dogs, and cattle. We fished, duck hunted, and quail hunted between the rice fields and cattle pastures. After school, we hauled hay and stacked it in

Billy's father's barn for eight cents a bale, which we split even. Our goal was 100 bales each day after school. It only took a couple of hours.

I got the best end of that deal since Billy's Dad furnished us with a tractor and hay trailer and paid for the gas. We each could make four bucks a day after school. A new pair of Levis only costs around three dollars.

Billy's Dad, JW Adams, was a cattleman and rice farmer. He had to be rich because he bought Billy a new red Ford Fairlane when he got old enough to get a driver's license.

And the first color TV I ever saw was in their home. No one but rich folks had a color TV. My Dad bought a black and white TV with a remote control named Randy.

Few teenagers owned an automobile in those days. Billy was the only person I knew who owned a new one our age.

I never had to ride Eugene "Jeep" Mitchell's bus 19 again to school.   Billy never asked me for a dime for gas. Three of those dimes would buy a gallon of regular.   That included cleaning your windshield, vacuuming your floors, and checking the air in your tires.

Standing Billy Adam and Kay Evans
Sitting Beverly Rieger and Randy Willis
Cappy Muchowich's home in Freeport, Texas

Billy Adam's car had a 4-track built-in cartridge player.
I'd never seen one. We must have listened to The Animals'
House of the Rising Sun 500 times, driving up and down
Surfside Beach. Soon, the 8-track would become the wave of
the future.

☆   ☆   ☆

CHAPTER 17
DUDE GOODRUM
A COWBOY'S COWBOY

When Mr. Adams hired Dude Goodrum as his foreman, Billy and I learned more about being a cowboy. Mr. Goodrum was inducted into the Texas Rodeo Cowboy Hall of Fame in 2001. He sat in a saddle like no other person I'd ever seen—like he was sculpted into the saddle and horse.

You could immediately tell he was the real deal. We'd all heard of him when he was working for Frank Harris's T-Diamond Ranch near West Columbia. I first saw him as a pickup man for Mr. Harris at the BCFA rodeo in Angleton. Mr. Harris also produced the annual state champion high school rodeo in Hallettsville.

Dude Goodrum was a Cowboy's Cowboy and friend. I admired him and looked up to him. He was a hero of mine.

Mr. Goodrum once roped a bull during a dance at the Brazoria County Fairgrounds. During the Brazoria County Rodeo next door, Mr. Goodrum was responsible for roping the bulls after they had been ridden.

When a "bad" bull jumped the rodeo arena fence, Dude Goodrum chased him down as he entered the nearby fairground dance hall. He roped and dragged him out of the packed dance hall and back to the rodeo arena. A lot of dancers were doing the Texas two-step that night. No one was injured. A good cowboy can save your life.

Great Cowboys had reputations like rock stars then. Dude Goodrum was one of the two best cowboys I've ever known. The other was my Dad, Jake Willis. Dude's son, Earl Goodrum, became good friends with Billy and me.

Like Dude and Billy, he was a lot better cowboy than me. Billy roped calves in high school rodeos. Earl rode bulls. I saw Earl ride a bull once in Angleton and decided that was not my gig. He rode him the full eight seconds, too. Not bad for a young man in high school.

Rex Bailey Jr.'s son Rex III and Babe Scotts's son Pruitt Scott were close friends to Billy and me. Rex had known Billy before our school days. Pruitt Scott was only one day younger than me. Billy was a year younger. I met Billy and Pruitt on the same day in Danbury in 1960. Rex Bailey III and Billy and I were as thick as thieves. I should have sent them monthly checks to keep them quiet about me.

Billy Adams and I played football together at Angleton High. He was the quarterback, and I was a defensive right tackle. I soon learned girls were more attracted to quarterbacks than tackles. It didn't hurt if they owned a new car and were better looking.

Later, when I got into the music biz, I learned girls had LSD—Lead Singer's Disease. "Quarterback Disease" was as prevalent then as it is today. Tom Brady was not the first to prove that if you're a drummer or defensive tackle, good luck. It's best to get yourself a color TV, one with remote control.

Billy was shy and humble. Everyone admired that. Billy was one of the stars when Angeton won the state championship in track. He could run like a deer. As I mentioned before, Coach Carl Davis said I ran fast. He added that the only problem was I ran too long in one place.

Our coaches had a way of encouraging you back then. I'm shocked I haven't been in counseling ever since. The truth is I loved Coach Davis's humor. He never meant anyone any harm. I've "borrowed" many of his sayings.

As I said before, we lived three miles from Angleton. The Old Danbury Road was where every local teenager went parking, although few admitted it. If you're under age 150, ask your parents what that means. When we got to be in our late teens, Billy and I would crank up Daddy's old Ford pickup. We didn't dare take Billy's fancy car. We illegally spotlighted and shot rabbits late at night from the dusty marine shell roads.

It was foggy one night when we came upon a couple "parking." We got the bright idea (pun intended) that we should turn around and turn off the headlights, and when we came alongside their car, we would spotlight their backseat.

109

We ran into them as we tried to locate their '57 Chevy in the dense fog. We fled as fast as those rabbits ran before the driver could crawl into the front seat and turn around.

I drove the old Ford pickup as quickly as it would go into Daddy's barn and prayed the driver or sheriff did appear. That ended my spotlighting days, at least for parkers.

Now you know why I love the movie *American Graffiti*. I never dreamed I'd miss getting up at 5:00 am, saddling a half dozen horses, and working twelve hours in the mosquitos, water moccasin, and rattlesnake-infested Saltgrass Country, not to mention the sweltering heat—but I do.

Randy Willis #76 and Billy Adams #12
Front Row Far Right
Coach Fred Johnson Back Row Right

CHAPTER 18
ANGLETON FOOTBALL
THE VALLEY OF DECISION

My Dad taught me to drive farm equipment when I was ten.

I started driving tractors at age ten.
I was 14 in this photo with Daddy.

Getting a driver's license was not that hard for me in Coach Nalbro Frazier's Driver's Education class.

Coach Frazier would stop under an oak tree next to Angleton Junior High (Central Elementary today) during Driver's Ed each day and roll down the windows. We all sat there enjoying the breeze under the giant shade tree for five or ten minutes. It was as if he was saying to slow down and enjoy the experience. The tree still stands there on East Cedar Street just east of North Valderas, next to the track and the old football stadium where I learned to play football.

Coach Frasier was the best coach I ever had. He once surprised me by sitting beside me in the Angleton High School gym near the top row of the basketball stands watching a basketball game and said, "Don't let him get to you," as Head Coach Fred Johnson walked by a half dozen rows below. That was the most encouraging advice a coach ever gave me.

Photograph Compliments of Angleton Times

Coaching Staff

Front row: Ronald Hoenig, Carl Davis, Jerry Brader, Herman Moore, Bill Lierman. Second row: Henry Hair, Norman Cobb, Charles McLeod, Nalbro Frasier, Fred Slough.

Coach Nalbro Frazier is on the top row, 3rd from the right. This was a wonderful group of coaches.

Randy Willis 1967, age 17
Angleton High School

I never considered any coach too hard. None of them were as hard as Daddy was on me. Daddy taught me always to be respectful and fair. He never told me to expect the same in return, but I noticed he always did. So, I did, too—I still hope for the same. But as the years have rushed by, I've learned it's best to let it go. That is unless when it concerns my children and grandchildren being mistreated. Then, the Biblical admonition of turning the other cheek requires time, prayer, and more time, and more prayer. And—you get the idea.

Angleton Coaches C. E. "Cotton" Peterson, Carl Davis, Fred Slough, Bill Hollas, Nalbro Frazier, and others I admired taught me a lot, and they were all fair men that I respected. Their motivational skills varied, though.

Coach Carl Davis was the most "colorful." "Willis, you're so clumsy you trip over the center line" [on the basketball court]. And, "Willis, the problem with you is you drink too much "Sweet Lucy" (aka water).

My water consumption was also a problem with Head Coach Fred Johnson. He took it as insubordination. It began during two-a-day football practices. We were allowed an 8-ounce empty Coke bottle filled with water halfway through each practice. By then, the water was hot from being exposed to the heat from the sun. No concern, though, because he also insisted we take salt tablets.

In fairness to our coaches, this was the protocol almost everywhere. From antiquity to the late 1960s, athletes were advised not to drink during exercise since fluid ingestion was believed to impair athletic performance. Water would slow you down. Publications soon began to warn of the dangers of dehydration, citing illnesses and deaths. I first heard about the shift from salt tablets to sports drinks in the early '70s. By then, I was in college.

Later, another coach and friend would teach me fairness and respect for others like my Dad and Coach Frasier had.

114

His name was Darrell Royal.   He once said, "The real make of a man is how he treats people who can do nothing for him."

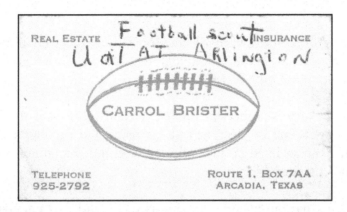

The first person to recruit me to play college football was Coach Burley Bearden, head coach at the University of Texas at Arlington. Coach Bearden was told about me by Carrol Brister, a football scout from Arcadia, Texas. Arcadia was also the home of my brother Buddy. He and Buddy were friends.

Coach Bearden met my Dad and me at the Taco House. The greasy spoon restaurant was on Highway 35, with a jukebox constantly playing Roy Orbison's hits.   Daddy and I ate breakfast there often.   The price was low enough, and the food was not half bad.   And we both liked Roy Orbison— although three songs in a row was enough. I think of that every time I watch *Pretty Woman* on TV, which has only been two or three times.

Coach Bearden began, "Coach Fred Johnson will not recommend you." That night, he offered me a scholarship, so whatever Coach Johnson told him was not a deal-breaker. And I'm sure my brother Buddy informed the scout I was no longer on Coach Johnson's Christmas card list. But it made

115

me wonder why the next school recruited me, knowing Coach Johnson would not endorse me.

I soon discovered few other colleges had heard of me. They became aware of me by watching films of games provided by Coach Johnson that showed how great my teammate Larry Webb was.

Larry was the star linebacker and fullback with all the awards, and he deserved all of them, but he was also the linebacker lined up just a few feet behind me, an unheralded defensive tackle.

I had no awards, but I was 6' 5" and 210 pounds and almost impossible to miss on film if you were scouting Larry. Contrary to Coach Davis's joke, he later said I was fast for a lineman, whatever that meant.

I learned much later that the great Texas college football coaches and recruiters knew more about the integrity of high school coaches than they did the players they were recruiting. They would go the extra mile to consider a high school player recommended by a coach they respected and trusted. I did not have that advantage, but I had Larry Webb lined up behind me on film.

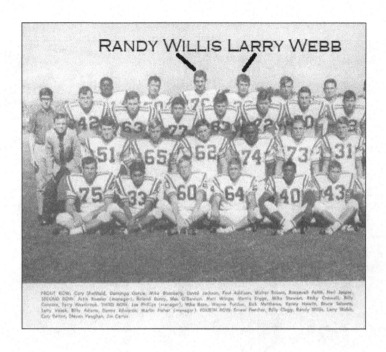

RANDY WILLIS LARRY WEBB

FRONT ROW: Cory Sheffield, Domingo Garcia, Mike Blumberg, David Jackson, Paul Addison, Walter Brown, Roosevelt Robb, Neil Jenson. SECOND ROW: Artie Keeler (manager), Roland Surey, Mac O'Banion, Bert Winge, Harris Diggs, Mike Stewart, Ricky Crowell, Billy Connors, Terry Westbrook. THIRD ROW: Joe Phillips (manager), Mike Ross, Wayne Purdue, Rick Matthews, Randy Hewitt, Bruce Schoate, Larry Vasek, Billy Adams, Danny Edwards, Martin Fisher (manager). FOURTH ROW: Ernest Fletcher, Billy Clegg, Randy Willis, Larry Webb, Cary Barton, Steven Vaughan, Jim Carter.

★   ★   ★

I first watched The University of Texas play football at my friend Billy Adam's home. As I mentioned, Billy Adam's family owned a Color TV. That was a big deal then; ours was black and white. That night, I became a fan of Duke Carlisle. He was the first college football player I ever became a fan. That night, I also became a fan of University of Texas football. I was only thirteen.

Several years later, during my junior year of high school in the Fall of 1966, Coach Carl Davis walked into the Angleton gym while we practiced basketball. He announced over the weekend that he had seen the best high school running back he had ever seen during the state playoffs. His name was Steve Worster from Bridge City. Bridge City had beaten Conroe 41-17 in the 3A Bi-district game. Angleton was a 3A school, too.

117

Randy Willis, age 16, dunking the basketball.
Angleton High School

If we had won our district, we would have played Bridge City. Back then, Texas had only four classifications in high school sports, with 4A being the biggest. Coach Davis was not the only coach in the stands during that game.   We soon learned that Darrell K Royal, Head Football Coach of The University of Texas, was as impressed by Worster as Carl Davis.

I followed Worster's next games in the news to see if the Conroe game was a fluke. Bridge City next handled Clear Creek, 36-7, before defeating San Marcos, 28-7.

I also knew that would all soon end when Bridge City faced the top-ranked team in the state, unbeaten McKinney. They had the best defense in the state and shut teams down all year. During the playoffs, McKinney had given up seven points in three games.

Steve Worster proved unstoppable and carried the ball 36 times for 249 yards and three touchdowns, leading his team to an impressive 30-6 win over previously unbeaten McKinney. Now, the stage was set to see which of the more than 75 colleges offers nationwide he would accept.

Because of Worster's choice and Duke Carlisle, I became the biggest Texas Longhorn fan on this side of the Colorado River.

A year later, Leon Manley recruited Larry Webb and me to play football at the University of Texas on the same day during a visit to Angleton High School. Larry and I were friends. We duck hunted and fished together in the rice fields surrounding my parent's farmhouse on 40 acres and the Brazoria County Saltgrass Country on weekends.

Coach Manley and Angleton High School counselor John Craven told me I would need to take additional algebra courses that summer to be admitted to the University of Texas. They had it all planned out. I could take these courses at Alvin Junior College, only 20 miles away. UT

119

would accept the credits from Alvin Junior College. The college was state-supported, so the tuition was reasonable.

Coach Fred Johnson was not in the meeting. I had no clue why they recruited me at the time, knowing that Coach Royal sought high school coaches' recommendations. And knowing Johnson would never recommend me.

A decade later, in 1978, *Texas Monthly* published a story about Coach Johnson entitled "The Great Rockdale Mutiny." The article reads in part, "Fred Johnson has been a high school football coach, and on the record, a very good one. Eighteen of those years, taking whatever talent has come to him in towns like Mission, Kerrville, Gonzales, Angleton, and Rockdale, he has turned in winning seasons. Last year, Johnson's teams won state championships in football and track. This year, he is out of a job."

The article continued: "But this was no ordinary coaching ouster. Johnson resigned after every team member signed a petition asking for his dismissal, and the resulting upheaval, replete with overtones of ideology and class, has threatened to tear this Central Texas town apart."

Johnson was quoted in the article as saying, "Players learn the willingness to give their time, accept strict rules, and subordinate themselves for the good of the team. Some don't and can't accept those things and become failures."

His words rang familiar. Ten years before the Rockdale High School Mutiny, Fred Johnson insisted I meet in his office to discuss my insubordination. He explained that he had done his best with me but had resigned to the fact that he had failed and I would always be a loser. His words did not discourage me but had the opposite effect.

★　　　★　　　★

More severe events soon showed me how silly and petty all this was. My sainted grandmother died in 1973. I adored her.

That same year, Willie Nelson moved to Austin at the suggestion of his friend Darrell Royal. Soon, tragedy hit the Royals. Coach and Edith Royals' daughter, an aspiring artist, was killed in a bus accident. Willie couldn't find the words until he played the *Healing Hands of Time* for Coach Royal.

Nine years later, Willie would sing it again when the Royals' son David, a musician, died in a motorcycle accident. Willie sang the song again at Coach Royals' funeral with tears in his eyes in 2012.

The *Healing Hands of Time* is my second favorite Willie Nelson song. My favorite is *In God's Eyes*.

The song begins:
"Never think evil thoughts of anyone
It's just as wrong to think as to say
For a thought is but a word that's unspoken
In God's eyes He sees it this way"

Fred Johnson was inducted into the Rockdale Sports Hall of Fame in 2011 and the Kerrville Tivy Hall of Fame, where he was a standout athlete. He was a U.S. Army veteran and a Rice University graduate who played football and ran track.

I was pleased to try and see him through God's eyes. Through God's eyes, he, like me, fell short of God's Glory. We all have feet of clay. In hindsight, his flaws fell short of mine. The *Healing Hands of Time* handles most things.

121

Top Row: Rex Baily, Torbett Clements, Randy Willis, Harold Hubbard, Joe Ford, and Coach Scheer. Second Row: Bill Bingham, David Hurta, Joe Hazelwood, Lindell Barham, Jim Brashear. Bottom Row: Mike Rose, T. J. Wright, Ron Thomas.

VARSITY BASKETBALL

Angleton — 23
Cy-Fair — 0

The Cypress-Fairbanks Bobcats came to Angleton hoping to avenge last year's defeat by the Wildcats, but only met disappointment at the hands of the sturdy Wildcat defense.

Angleton had a 20-0 lead at half time, but managed only a 24 yard field goal by Cary Sheffield the last half for the final 23-0 score. The Wildcat touchdowns came on a 7 yard run by Jasper, a 60 yard scamper by Edwards, and a 1 yard plunge by Larry Webb.

The Wildcat defense, led by Ernest Fletcher, Jimmy Carter, and Larry Webb, was superb as they blocked three punts, recovered a fumble, and intercepted a pass, completely stopping the Cy-Fair offense.

Steve Worster

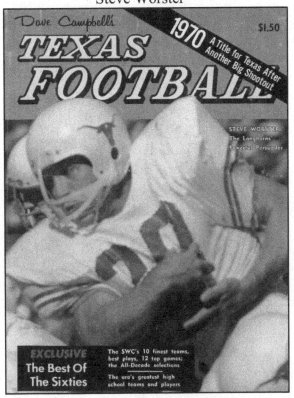

Angleton's Randy Willis
will be in action tonight
against Galveston Ball
at Angleton.
Photo by Doc Barganier

6' 5" and 16 years old

Randy Willis, age 16.
Angleton High School 1966

CHAPTER 19
LARRY WEBB

Larry Webb and I visited Austin and the UT campus unofficially. Larry said, "You want to meet Steve Wooster? He's a roommate with Jay Cormier from Freeport." Jay played high school football at Brazosport, just a few minutes south of Angleton.

"No thanks," I said, "I've got to meet a friend." She was a girl from Austin who often visited her mother in Angleton. We had a couple dates in Angleton, but Austin was a four-hour drive. I could not afford 32 cents a gallon for gas, and my tires were always threadbare.

When Larry and I met later, he said, "You should have come and met Worster.

I responded, "Let's see Larry, have lunch with my beautiful date, or meet Steve Wooster." When I got home the next day, I had second thoughts; I could have seen her again the next time she visited Angleton. I still regret that decision.

The truth is it had nothing to do with her. I was too shy and intimidated to meet my high school football idol. "Big Woo," Steve Worster soon became the cornerstone of the Texas Longhorn's famed Wishbone offense. I never met him. He died on August 13, 2022. I'm still a fan.

Junior Senior Prom Penney Skaggs and Randy Willis

I also never took the needed math classes due to my parents' divorce two months after Coach Manley's visit. In those days, divorce was a huge deal. No one in my family had ever divorced in our known family history. I was devastated when I saw my mother's tears. They had been married for 20 years.

After college, Larry Webb and I stayed in touch until about a decade before his tragic death. I suddenly lost track of him. After college, he worked with Pelican's Wharf Restaurant in Austin and later in San Antonio. I ate at both several times to visit Larry.

Larry played on two of UT's National Champion football teams. Larry was a better player than me. Those teams had more talent than I'd ever seen. I would have never started, but the bench was not a bad seat to watch the games, and what an honor it would have been, not to mention the financial advantages of a scholarship. I had no money.

Larry Webb died on February 3, 2019. He'd been suffering for four or five years from Chronic traumatic encephalopathy (CTE). CTE is a progressive and fatal brain disease associated with repeated traumatic brain injuries (TBIs), including concussions and repeated blows to the head. He ultimately died of Renal Cell Carcinoma while in hospice care. I miss him.

☆   ☆   ☆

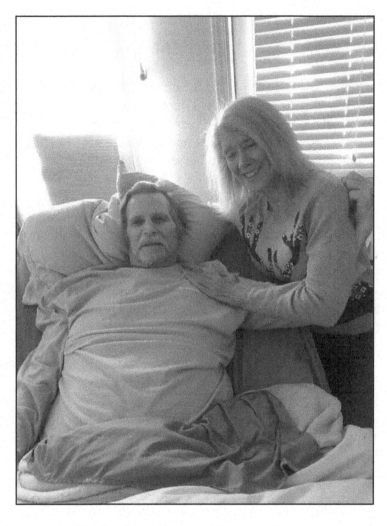

Larry Webb and his faithful wife, Mary Jane, to the end.

CHAPTER 20
BETTY MACIK

My love of the theater began at Angleton High School. My excitements were few when I was raised on a 40-acre farm on the Old Danbury Road. Work seemed to always be competing with hunting and fishing. Fooling around with horses was my addiction, at least at the beginning of my teens.

The day's excitement was watching my one-eyed Catahoula Leopard Dog Bob bark as I sat on my Dad's pickup tailgate.

A movie now and then at the Surf Drive-in near Clute was the "big time." But my Dad's ole rusty Ford pickup had no trunk to hide in.

The Lake Theater in Lake Jackson was the mountain top. This was before the Beacon Theater opened in Angleton.

Watching a play at Angleton High School with my friends in it was incredible. I was amazed at how much talent they had. I've loved the theater ever since. I could not guess how often I've seen my favorite *Les Misérables*.

I've been trained in creative writing not to use adjectives (Hemingway) and never use adverbs that end in "ly" (Stephen King). And use only [sorry delete only] short sentences and omit unnecessary words (Jerry B. Jenkins). Jerry clapped his hands (omit his hands).

I will adhere to all of the above today except using adjectives. How can I not use an adjective or two or three when writing about Betty Macik?

It's been over 10 years since Betty Macik died on March 12, 2013. Betty graduated from Angleton High School with me.

I won't write about her career because she never spoke of it. But she was an excellent actress in high school, college, and Hollywood. After spending years in the industry, she called me one day and asked if she could stop by my home in Wimberley and visit on her way to Angleton.

When she arrived, she said, "I had to leave; there is so much decadence there." I never asked her what she meant by that, but I offered to drive back and get her belongings. She said her Dad had offered to do the same. And he did. I'm glad he did because I might not have been cordial to Betty's former beau, Randy Quaid.

We became close friends. We never dated. She was way out of my league in charm, grace, and beauty—inside and out. But we were close friends and spoke on the phone as long as her health permitted.

After a visit to her home in Angleton on today's Hospital Drive (East County Road 341), our primary conversation was about her home, which she was finishing out on the inside. I could not help her with that because of the distance, but I did volunteer to help build her chicken coops. How much time and enjoyment you can spend on such a project with a friend is immeasurable.

After 911, she painted me a scene from the tragedy. It hangs at the top of my stairway. I often think of her when I walk up those stairs—never when I step down.

Betty was a devout Catholic and loved Jesus. Most of our telephone conversations were about what was happening in our lives but always included Christ.

She called me one day when she lost her job at Brazos Mall, "They fired me when they discovered I have cancer," she said. That broke my heart. And it still does as I write that sentence. I'm unsure of any other details; that's all she said. In fairness to Brazos Mall, Betty was on painkillers and heavy medication by then. She only mentioned it once. She seemed overwhelmed and also said, "I look so old." I assured her she still was beautiful. And she was, inside and out.

As her health declined, we spoke more about Heaven. We stayed clear of religion. We got down to where the rubber meets the road. What did the Word of God say about Heaven? What did it say about being born again? When she died, she was at peace and had the security of knowing where she would spend the rest of eternity. No, not because of me or religion, but because of the promises in the Word of God she stood on, claimed, and accepted and the still, small voice that comforted her. Bound For Glory.

She was a beautiful soul—I miss her. I bet she would be a star if there were a theater in Heaven. I can't wait to see her performance. I'm sure she plays the part of an angel, perhaps Gabriel, for that's the angel who always brings good news.

Betty Macik, *Bound For Glory* 1976
Her stage name was Elizabeth Macey.

Betty's Signature Elizabeth A. Macik

Betty painted this for me as a Thanksgiving
gift after 911.

BAND SWEETHEART
Betty Macik

Two wonderful friends, Betty Macik and Kathy Copeland

AARON WILLIS, FAMILY & RANDY WILLIS
Les Misérables - Bass Concert Hall

Alana, Presley, Baylee, Aaron, and Randy Willis
My favorite play, *Les Misérables*.
Bass Concert Hall, Austin, Texas

✫   ✫   ✫

CHAPTER 21
JAKE WILLIS AND DOW CHEMICAL

The A.P. Beutel Building was designed to house 400 Dow Chemical scientists, engineers, and executives. Houston's foremost interpreters of famed Frank Lloyd Wright, MacKie, and Kamrath were recommended to the Dow Chemical Company in 1950 by Alden B. Dow, an architect who studied under Wright and was also the son of the founder of Dow Chemical, Herbert Henry Dow.

Dr. A.P. "Dutch" Beutel became the first general manager of Dow's Texas Division, located in Freeport.

Dr. Beutel designed a unique desk shaped like an artist's palette so he "could look each assistant in the eye."

On the day this group photo was taken in 1968, a round table was used so each man could look the other in the eye, evidenced by the gentleman seated on the far right looking at a "hayseed" cowboy with only a high school education named Jake Willis—my Dad.

His name was Joel Franklin Monroe (Levi) Leathers. In 1941, he began as a second-class oiler in the Dow

137

powerhouse. He became general manager of the Texas Division in 1966. The year this photo was taken in 1998, he became director of operations for Dow Chemical U.S.A. and executive vice-president of Dow U.S.A. in 1971. Like Dr. Beutel, he was fair and one of the most brilliant minds in the chemical industry.

But on this day, another oversaw the negotiations with the unions. In 1968, my father headed the largest union at Dow, the International Union of Operating Engineers, Local 564, during the collective bargaining. Dow employed 6,390 men and women in Plants A and B in Brazoria County. The new General Manager as of 1968 was David Rooke.

Top row fourth from the right (tall man with glasses), Howard McNair was the first to call Daddy "Jake."

David Rooke was another excellent and fair man. He used the ratchet wrench as a symbol for his employees:

138

"Always forward, never back." He was named President of Dow Chemical USA in 1978.

These men cared about the well-being of their employees and were fair in negotiating. Levi Leathers, a research and development pioneer, was passionate about safety.

A union strike was held at Dow during a cold and rainy winter in years past. Dr. Beutel ordered rubber boots for the strikers on the picket line and some scrap lumber so they could build a fire to stay warm. When asked why he did that, he responded, "Those fellows were my men before they went on strike, and they'll be my men when it's over."

Another story in this group photo is when contracts were signed between Dow's executives and the union's representatives. This story perhaps matters little to anyone except me, my three sons, and six grandchildren.

The tall gentleman standing 4th from the right with glasses is Howard McNair. Mr. McNair was the major manager of Chlor-Alkali Production at the Freeport Plant. He became Daddy's close friend, as did many of the men in the photo.

Mr. McNair was the person who nicknamed Daddy "Jake," saying you remind me of a real-life John Wayne. Many people made that observation, but Daddy was never flattered. John Wayne did not enlist in the service, as many other movie stars did, during World War II. In fact, most of the men in this photo served in the military.

It was a primary reason that the atmosphere was mutual respect, politeness, and empathy when they negotiated. Now grant you, Daddy could charm the pants off a mule.

139

Late in Daddy's life, he drove out to a pasture to watch his horses as the sunset. He was recovering from cancer. His pickup got stuck in the mud. Daddy was hardheaded and refused to buy a new invention called the cell phone. He would have to make the long hike through the woods in the dark to the country road and hope someone would give him a ride. They did, which is what most people did in those days in Brazoria County.

When Mr. McNair heard the news, he bought Daddy a cell phone, paid well in advance for the service, and delivered it to him, saying, "This is not to be negotiated, Jake; carry this phone," Mr. McNair said.

Randy Willis engagement photo.

During my senior year at Southwest Texas State University, I met a girl in Common's Cafeteria dressed in her Strutters outfit. As a "goodwill ambassador" of SWT, I decided to follow her and make small talk. I soon discovered she was from Lake Jackson. After we became engaged, and on my first visit to her home, I met her neighbor on Oyster Creek's banks.

His name was Howard McNair. He and his family attended our wedding. She is the mother of my three sons— the best three boys this side of the Brazos—*make that the Mississippi*. We divorced after 15 years, primarily due to my shortcomings.

141

★   ★   ★

But none of this mattered to me in the summer of '68 in Brazoria County's Salt Grass Country as I shoved levees in the rice fields 12 hours a day for a mere eight dollars for Babe Scott in the sweltering heat with water moccasins every few yards crawling between my long legs and my tall rubber boots.

Mr. Scott had a gentleman named Humble with whom I worked. We napped daily in a shed for an hour after devouring a sack lunch at his instruction.

One day, driving to a rice field, Mr. Humble said to me out of the blue, "Your Daddy sure raised ya right."

"What do you mean," I asked.

"You always say yes sir, no sir, thank you sir to me. Most white boys don't say that to black folks."

It was one of the greatest compliments of my life. Mr. Humble once stopped with me in the Salt Grass Country. "Let me show ya something," he said.

He took a shovel from the back of Babe Scott's old rusty pickup and pointed to some tin roofing in a pile that Hurricane Carla had blown there years before.

On top of the siding was a colossal rattlesnake basking in the sun. He walked about 20 feet from the snake, flipped the shovel like a pocket knife, and hit him dead center. He turned and walked back to the truck with a smile.

"How did you learn to do that?" I asked.

"Oh, you pick it up after a few hundred tries."

"Yes, sir," I said, but I thought I'd rather face a den of rattlesnake than him in a knife fight. I was also glad I'd been calling him sir.

☆   ☆   ☆

But, little did I know that, through the most unexpected circumstances, Dow Chemical Company would get me out of the rice fields and, trailing on a horse, the south end of a northbound cow. And yes, later, pay for almost every dime my college education cost.

Dow did all this by turning me down for a job during negotiations of '68. But I thought you said, Randy, I'm getting to that in the next chapter.

I overheard Daddy on the phone one night at home in high school. I figured the man on the other end was a friend of Daddy until he said, "The only reason your son Jerry has become a Superintendent [at Dow Chemical] is because he has been brown-nosing Dow's big shots."

Daddy paused and responded slowly but clearly, "I will tell him you said that. And if he doesn't whip your ass, I'm going to whip his ass."

He was a cowboy's cowboy and a man's man. I miss him.

Julian Willis World War II

☆　　☆　　☆

CHAPTER 22
SOUTHWEST TEXAS STATE
~~COLLEGE~~ UNIVERSITY SAN MARCOS, TEXAS
1968-1972

I'd seen the world by the time I completed my book learning at Angleton High School—if you mean the world is the south end of a northbound cow.

What do all of these have in common: movie stars walking around town half-naked, a former President of the United States teaching a government class, a flood that reached the third floor of an apartment community, a college president forced to resign, ten people arrested and kicked out of college for protesting the war.

And a strange cigarette rolled in tiny papers, a draft lottery that might determine if you live or die, a hundred beautiful young women strutting around town in outfits I'd never seen on the farm, a chili cook-off with 50,000 folks in attendance, yet bared women chefs? I surmised the next thing you know, they'd want to vote.

☆　　☆　　☆

The Southwest Texas State University Strutters.
The home in the background was built in 1896 and
was moved to campus. It is where LBJ resided as a
student at SWT (Texas State University).

And a fraternity I became a member of by the strangest
set of circumstances, and dare I say, panty raids have in
common?

The answer is the next four-plus years of my life, also
known as college. And yes, an occasional class that expanded
my horizons, but not my common sense, like the marriage
class Dr. Azalete Little taught that I can't remember the name
of or a single lesson. I suppose that's why I'm single.

No, I never strung ladies' underwear like Indian scalps
out my dorm window on a clothesline. I was much too
dignified, i.e., shy, for that; besides, I had lived off campus
by then and couldn't afford a clothesline. Some women
students began throwing buckets of water out of their dorm
windows in protest. I didn't own a raincoat either.

146

Two years later, I missed the streaking craze, so I figured my conservative cowboy Southern Baptist credentials were still intact. I never knew how Mama and Daddy felt about any of the above since it slipped my mind to mention them.

☆   ☆   ☆

I never planned on going to college. My parents divorced the month after I graduated from Angleton High School in 1968. No one in my family had ever divorced, and no one had ever been to college.

I had several choices: join the military and train for Vietnam, work on a ranch or farm, get a job at Dow Chemical, which rapidly became not an option because of Vietnam, or try to get into a college just weeks before classes began with a high school resume that included auto mechanics and athletics. I didn't even know how to spell algebra and still can't spell trigonometry.

My mother moved from our home on Old Danbury Road to 113 Hargett Street in Clute, Texas, after their divorce. Her tiny home was within walking distance of Clute City Hall on the main street. After sundown, I decided to take a walk. I stopped and sat under a giant oak tree in front of the Clute City Hall. I sat there for an hour contemplating my choices. I could not decide.

The following month, my friend Glen Hardwick from high school asked if I'd like to ride with him to Garner State Park on the 4th of July. "Several of our friends will be there," he said. We headed to Garner. Glen was a year older than me and had been a freshman that year at Southwest Texas State College (SWT) in San Marcos.

147

Glen was living in Jackson Hall, which had opened the year before. It was the highest building on campus and in Hays County (and still is), with the Victory Star atop the 11-story building. Glen's father, M. Warren Hardwick, M.D., was a doctor in Angleton. I was a dirt-poor farm boy, and Jackson Hall was way beyond my aspirations. I had no money saved for college.

On the way to Garner State Park, Glen said he'd like to show me the campus and Jackson Hall. I was in awe of Old Main and the San Marcos River. He said you should enroll. I said, "Sure, registration is just weeks away, and I have no money. Where would I live?"

I was resigned to the fact that it was impossible. Glen said, "You never know until you try. The worst thing they can do is say no. They can't shoot you." So, I figured I'd try after I got home from Garner State Park, knowing my chances were slim and none.

Glen and I continued to Garner to meet with friends from Angleton and Brazosport. We camped at his parent's ranch nine miles north of Leakey, Texas, near Garner. The next day, I spent much of the day hanging out with a friend who was an aspiring singer.

We met a few years before at Garner when I was seated at a Garner State Park picnic table. I asked him if he minded singing a song. I had heard he was good. He nodded and began singing Marty Robins's *You Gave Me a Mountain*.

I asked him his name. "John Rodriguez," he said. We became friends. He changed his name twice over the next couple of years and took off to Nashville to see if he could make it into country music.

148

John Rodriguez and Randy Willis
Garner State Park. Easter 1969

☆   ☆   ☆

I contacted the Office of the Registrar after I got home from Garner. They explained that I must take an American College Testing (ACT) exam.

They also added that the only room left on campus was in Harris Hall. It was the only room in the building where three people were allowed to live because it was at the end of the building and oversized.

It looked as if it had seen better days. I found out later that it was the first male dorm on campus, built in 1937. Someone had withdrawn from school, probably after seeing that room.

149

I told my Dad I needed to borrow $400 if accepted by the college. He agreed, saying, "You can pay me back when you become a big shot." In other words, he never expected to see that money again.

The room was sure to go quickly. College registrations were soaring across America due to college deferments from the draft. I took the ACT and earned the lowest score allowed to enter SWT. I believe it was 14. The room was still available, and my path was cleared to attend college. I was happy as a Colt in Clover.

I explained to my two new roommates that I wasn't much of a student in high school. One was from Rockdale and was there because of Vietnam, and the other was from Austwell-Tivoli on the Texas Gulf Coast. He looked smart, so I asked, "What rank did you graduate in your class?"

"Ninth," he said. Wow, I'm in trouble, I thought.

"How many students were in your graduating class?"

"Ten."

The pressure was off. But I still had to ask, "Who graduated tenth?"

"My twin brother," he smiled. I didn't dare ask where he enrolled in college.

Every time we drive to Port Aransas for a break, I tell my three sons and six grandchildren that story. They finished it for me as soon as I mentioned Austwell-Tivoli. Today, their version is better than mine.

150

Front row: Alana, Baylee, Jessah, with Juliette, Olivia, Josh, and Adam Willis. Back Row: Presley, Aaron, and Corbin Willis. Jessah is pregnant with Violet Willis.

☆　　　☆　　　☆

On the first day in Harris Hall, someone called my room and told me the Dean of Students needed to talk to me—immediately. There was a big problem with my registration. "It may be disallowed."

It was a long, agonizing walk from Harris Hall up the steep hill on the other side of campus to Old Main and the office of the Dean of Students, Floyd Martine. I reckoned I was off to the rice fields again—not in Brazoria County—but in Vietnam.

I arrived just before they closed. There was a room full of staff, including the Dean. I explained I had received the call, and here I am.

They all began to laugh. "Son, that's an old joke," the Dean smiled, "that the upperclassmen play on incoming first-year students. You're the 30th in the last couple hours to climb this hill."

I was so relieved that the thought of being upset never crossed my mind. I never found out who made the call, but I did think it was strange that Glen Hardwick never warned me and that the person who called had my name and room number. It didn't matter; I was a college student. The first in our family.

I would see a much different landscape during the first week at Southwest Texas State College (University the following year). The San Marcos River flowed by the campus. Swimming and floating in the river was in my budget, too—free. I could buy a meal card for the semester and my tuition, which was less than $175 for a full-time student.

The $325.00 meal card allowed me to eat at Commons and Jones Cafeterias. It was just a stamp on my college ID but a life savior. At least I would not go hungry. I suspect they lost money on me.

Mama bought me a used Volkswagen that cost $400 and had 36 horsepower. It was the only tiny car with enough headroom to fit my 6'5" frame. Wilt Chamberlain, 7'1", did Volkswagen's commercials.

Wilt Chamberlain was a center in the National
Basketball Association for 14 seasons.

Joe Birch, our old neighbor on Coleman Street in Clute from the 50s, painted the used Volkswagen in his garage fire engine red at my request for $200, which was high, but I was in a hurry. The red paint dripped down the driver's door. I asked him if he would repaint that part of the door. "For another $80, I will," He said. I passed on his offer.

CHAPTER 23
Brazosport Junior College & Dow

Go figure, I ran out of money after one semester. But, a brand new junior college opened in the fall of 1968 in Freeport, Texas, just south of Angleton. It was named Brazosport Junior College. Classes were held at the Brazosport Education Center in Freeport. Two years later, Brazosport Junior College became Brazosport College and graduated its first 25 students.

Today, Brazosport College has an enrollment of almost 4,000 and was named a top 10 community college in the nation in 2015 by Aspen Institute. But, all I was concerned about in 1969 was whether SWT would accept the college credits I'd earned at Brazosport Junior College, and they did because the college founders were way ahead of me on that issue, as most all other issues.

After one semester and one summer working at Dow Chemical as an Operating Engineer, i.e., janitor (Sanitation Engineer on my résumé) from 3 p.m. to 11 p.m. Monday through Friday, I saved enough money to return to SWTSU. I was back in the saddle.

☆   ☆   ☆

During Easter in 1969, I became friends with Diane Gray from Brazosport while visiting Garner State Park. Her father was a medical doctor and friends with Glen Hardwick's father, M. Warren Hardwick, MD, from Angleton.

Diane and I hung out during the summer of '69. Knowing I did not own a TV, she invited me to her father's home on the San Bernard River near Freeport, Texas, to

154

watch the first landing on the Moon. Glen was with me. We were all transfixed, as was the rest of the world.

The landing on the surface of the Moon occurred on July 20, 1969. Astronaut Neil Armstrong confirmed the landing to Mission Control and the world with the words, "Houston, Tranquility Base here. The *Eagle* has landed." But all was not tranquil in Diane's life. She was my first friend to die young. She would not be the last.

If I lived to 200, I could never thank Brazosport Junior College, Southwest Texas State University, or Dow Chemical Company enough for giving me the education and funds to see the light at the end of an impossible dream.

I returned two more summers to work shiftwork in the "hell hole" of Dow the mag-cells, removing magnesium cell sludge. I was a Sludger. It was great pay, but it took a lot of time and half an hour of overtime to reach my college budget.

It was the most demanding job I have ever done. Many of the "college boys" quit on the first day. The sludge became part of Mag Mountain, the highest point in the county. I would lose up to 16 pounds a day in water weight.

Dehydration, heat exhaustion, and heat stroke were ever-present. But then again, it wasn't any more challenging than working for my Dad. He always said, "It's not much for a high stepper." I'm still unsure what that meant and wasn't about to ask.

During my last summer at Dow, I was transferred to the Mag Cells, Magnesium Chloride (Mag-Clor). You had to wear a heavy cream over your exposed skin to keep the gas

155

from stinging. My foreman liked me. He called me into his office at noon, my last workday. It was also the last day of summer employment for all college boys.

My foreman said, "I want you to get your belongings and leave this plant—now!"

It was a long walk, and the buses did not run at noon, so I asked, "Why, have I done something wrong?"

He explained it was a tradition for the men on the last day of the college boys' summer employment to hold them down in the shower at the end of their shift and paint a particular part of their anatomy (my words, not his) with red spray paint.

I shook his hand, thanked him, decided not to shower, and made it to the clock room at the plant exit faster than Bob Hayes, the world's fastest human.

I purposed in my heart that no one would ever make me accept a "red paint job" again as Joe Birch did and, more importantly, the one I almost received at Dow.

How do I ensure I'm never in a position like that again?

The answer was to get an education. I was motivated, but it took 50 years for me to buy another red vehicle. And that was because of the nationwide shortage of trucks.

Today, I drive my red GMC pickup chasing the south end of a northbound cow and a horse or two or three with my grandkids in tow.

During my sophomore year, Southwest Texas State College became Southwest Texas State University. I changed the sticker on my back car window and was as proud as a peacock. I was now a university student like my friends in Austin on the famed 40 acres. I never knew what the difference was, but it sounded impressive.

The Lottery

The day 90 minutes changed my life and a half million others.

When I returned to Southwest Texas State University in San Marcos in the autumn of 1969, I ate peanut butter for lunch daily and red beans and rice for supper. I lost a lot of weight. But a more severe dilemma arose as winter approached.

December 1, 1969, my future as a student was again in doubt. The United States Senate passed President Richard Nixon's draft scheme the month before.

I was a 19-year-old sophomore with a glimmer of hope when a draft lottery decided my fate as a student. I can't win for losing, I thought.

I had just left a Brazoria County rice field two years before, and now it would appear I was headed to another rice field, but this time, a bunch of strangers would be shooting at me. I no longer thought the snakes and mosquitoes were that terrible in Brazoria County.

The lottery determined the draft order for induction into military service in the Vietnam War. Every qualifying male student was on pins and needles as we awaited our future

157

based on the luck of the draw. There would be no more student deferments from the draft.

I lived in a 30' travel trailer in Pecan Park RV Park on the San Marcos River near San Marcos. Gerald Thornton, the owner, agreed to a dollar a foot, $30 per month for the spot, which included water and electricity. There was also a pay phone, laundry, and shower house across the street. I needed all three.

I did not have a television or a nearby newspaper stand, so I drove on campus to Glen Hardwick's dorm early the next day, Buckner Hall, to read the lottery results. I never asked why Glen moved from Jackson Hall to Buckner Hall, but I figured even doctors' sons must budget. Glen was in ROTC (Reserve Officers' Training Corp), so his future military service was already set on a path.

A large glass container held 366 blue plastic balls containing every possible birth date and affected men between 18 and 26. The first "ping-pong ball" was drawn by Congressman Alexander Pirnie of the House Armed Services Committee.

The first birthdate Congressman Pirnie drew was September 14. A friend of mine was born on that date. He was a senior. He was soon drafted and forced to quit college. I never heard from him again.

After a year of struggling to attend college, I had everything in place, and now this curve ball has come out of Washington, DC, because of some "Domino Theory."

I began to scan the lottery drawing results at Buckner Hall from the Austin American Stateman posted in the lobby

158

on a bulletin board. The first 195 numbers drawn were called for military service almost immediately.

I scrolled down the list in tiny print and saw December 18, number 128. And then December 20, number 135. I had scrolled one box too far. Therefore, back up to December 19, my birthdate. It was number 240. The feeling I felt was beyond words. I spoke to no one. A few students were crying in the hallways and lobby.

I drove to the San Marcos River and sat under a massive Cypress Tree with my feet in the frigid water. Sitting under a tree has always been my city of refuge—a place to reflect. But, my emotions were not what I expected.

The guilt did not surprise me; I felt responsible for choosing college over serving my country, as several of my friends had died in Vietnam.

My father had fought on Iwo Jima in World War II. And so had every generation in my family, including World War I, the Civil War and the Revolutionary War.

Even with anti-war protests going on everywhere and the war at an all-time high for unpopularity, the guilt remained. I left the river for home with mixed emotions.

December 19 date was drawn number 240

After the lottery, Glen and I discussed renting a two-bedroom apartment at Malibu Apartments on Hopkins Street, although each entrance door was painted a different color.

Still, they wanted $100 monthly for a two-bedroom apartment with water and electricity included. I could not afford that, even with a roommate splitting the rent.

After working another summer at Dow, I could afford an apartment, and we were roommates for a year. It was my first apartment.

However, I soon discovered that medical doctors could afford maids. Glen grew up with a maid. He throws his dirty clothes in one corner and his clean clothes in another. And I don't believe he ever made a bed or washed a dish in his entire life. It drove me crazy.

Glen and I drove by Malibu Apartments a few years ago. It is still there with the same name. I suspect the rent may have gone up.

Glen allowed me to stay at his home in Angleton for my 25th class reunion two decades later. He was out of town. A 30-gallon trash can was in the middle of the living room filled with empty beer cans.

As I walked through his home, I discovered that the living room was the cleanest part of the house. I left a note that read, "Thank you, but no thank you. I got a motel room. The roaches are bigger than me in your kitchen."

I never wondered again why Glen remained a bachelor. I once hired maids; they were called my three sons.

Glen moved from the Malibu Apartments when he read in the San Marcos newspaper most car accidents occur within one mile of your home.

CHAPTER 24
Sigma Nu (ΣN) HT 139
SOUTHWEST TEXAS STATE UNIVERSITY

Sigma Nu (ΣN) Eta Tau Chapter at Southwest Texas State University, San Marcos, Texas, Randy Willis HT 139.

There ought to be a law against having that much fun — then again, there might have been.

Daddy loved Western fiction. His favorite writer was Zane Grey. They both idealized the American frontier.

A few years ago, I received a phone call from the Sigma Nu (ΣN) National Headquarters in Lexington, Virginia.

I was a Sigma Nu Fraternity member in college at Southwest Texas State University (Texas State University today) around the time of the Lincoln-Douglas debate.

Little did I know Zane Grey had been a Sigma Nu, too, in 1894, at the University of Pennsylvania. Sigma Nu was calling to request a copy of all my books. They wished to place them in their library next to Zane Grey's novels. They are there today. I was honored for more than one reason.

I gave my Grandson Corbin Willis a tour of Texas State University's campus in San Marcos a month ago, after our tradition of eating lunch at Kobe Steakhouse & Sushi hoping he would consider my alma mater. The best part of the tour for him was the soccer fields. My favorite was stopping in front of the ole Sigma Nu House near the soccer facilities. The house is a sorority house today.

My Grandson Corbin Willis, 2024, in front of the old Sigma Nu House, 401 Comanche Street, San Marcos, Texas. My room was the upstairs bay window on the far right.

I pointed out the upstairs bay window that was my room and fraternity brother Mark T. Davis's, too. I was the house manager, although Mark was the manager much longer. Our rent for the entire house, including a house (no longer there), outback was $500 monthly.

The house brought back a million memories.

I was first invited to the house when Glen Hardwick and I double-dated to Barn at York Creek, south of San Marcos on York Creek. It later burned. It was a Thursday night, nickel-beer night. That was all I could afford anyway. Sigma Nu Mark T. Davis was a bartender that night.

Someone announced they needed couples to volunteer to enter a kissing contest that would be judged by applause.

163

Hardwick volunteered my date and me. It was our first date. I'd just met her. There were four couples. We were third. As I kissed her as passionately as I could, the Sigma Nu's went crazy. We won the contest. The prize was a free pitcher of beer.

As I sat down, I thought I must be a great kisser!

Then Hardwick leaned over and whispered. "As you kissed her, your hand went up her back six inches." She was wearing the new craze, a micro mini-skirt. I told Glen it wasn't my fault. No one wore skirts that short at Angleton High School. She never knew why we won. And I wasn't about to tell her. The Sigma Nu's invited us to the Sigma Nu House for an after-party.

☆   ☆   ☆

After I became a Sigma Nu Active, one of my fraternity brothers asked if I would help him with his accounting homework. Accounting was my major. Bless his heart, as I parked in his apartment parking lot, a bunch of Sigma Nu pledges were hidden, waiting for me. My active fraternity brother had set me up.

They blindfolded me and another active they had already seized. They took us to a pasture in the middle of nowhere, stripped us butt naked, and left with all our clothes.

Once we got the blindfolds and ropes off our wrists, we decided to figure out where we were. After I climbed a very tall windmill, I could see the lights of IH 35 to the west and Gary Job Corp's lights to the east. Our only hope of not being arrested was to head toward a Mexican bar east on Highway 21.

We hid in the ditch across from the bar and waited until a male came out without a female. The first one that did laugh when we explained our dilemma. He said, "I will give you a ride. My friends will not believe this." Thank God there were no cell phones, especially those with cameras then.

When he dropped me off at the Sigma Nu House, the place was rockin' with a party. I ran through the front door and upstairs to my room as fast as Bob Hayes.

The Sigma Nu House

T.J. Goforth, who founded a town with his name in Hays County, built the Sigma Nu House at 401 Comanche Street, San Marcos, Texas, in ca 1905.

Eight years later, he sold the house to Thomas Green Harris. Harris was the first president of Southwest Texas State Normal School (known as Southwest Texas State College during my first year and Southwest Texas State University during my remaining years). And Texas State University today. Harris went to San Marcos Academy as its second president in 1911.

My first residence at SWT was Harris Hall, named after Thomas Harris. I would later live in his first residence, which was known as the Sigma Nu House at the time.

Harris Hall was the first male residence hall on Southwest State Teachers College's campus. Have you got all that? There will be a test later!

The Victorian-styled house with turned posts, fish scale shingles, pendants, and jigsawn brackets in the gable ends has a Historical Marker on its front porch erected by the Texas Historical Commission.

165

Yes, as I said, there ought to be a law against having that much fun—then again, there were—several of them.

SIGMA NU FRATERNITY, INC.

9 Lewis Street ♦ P. O. Box 1869 ♦ Lexington, Virginia 24450

Phone: (540) 463-1869 ♦ Fax: (540) 463-1669 ♦ E-mail: headquarters@sigmanu.org ♦ Website: www.sigmanu.org

October 24, 2015

Mr. Randy Willis

Dear Brother Willis,

I understand that you are the author of several history books. You may not know that the Richard R. Fletcher Memorial Library at Sigma Nu's headquarters in Lexington, Virginia, has an extensive collection of books that were authored by Sigma Nu initiates. These include works by Zane Grey (Penn Chapter), Wallace Stegner (Utah Chapter) and Dumas Malone (Emory Chapter), among many others. Many of these donated books are actually signed by the authors to Sigma Nu.

If you are so inclined, we would be happy to accept for inclusion in the Sigma Nu Authors Collection any or all of your works. There they will be available to educate future generations of young men who visit our headquarters. Many of the more recently published books have also been reviewed or mentioned in *The Delta* magazine for our readers.

I wish you success in your continuing writing efforts!

Very truly yours,

Robert A. McCully
Grand Historian, Sigma Nu Fraternity

bob_mccully @ comcast.net

I began to have a few more dates as I became comfortable with the Greek system of fraternities and sororities at Southwest Texas State University. The Sigma Nu's had their own table at Commons Dinning Hall, as did many social clubs.

Southwest Texas State University Homecoming. Me
with an Alpha Delta Pi member with a
Homecoming Sigma Nu (ΣN) Mum.

Steve McQueen

In 1972, my senior year at Southwest Texas State (Texas State), *The Getaway*, starring Steve McQueen, was filmed in San Marcos.

My fraternity brothers were used as extras since one of my brothers, Bill Fecci, wife, worked for the law firm handling the movie.

My fraternity brother Mark T. Davis became friends with McQueen's bodyguard. Mark said he was a former University of Texas football player (lineman) named Abbott. They were both native Americans. He could not remember his first name.

I googled Texas Longhorn Abbott and found Danny Abbott. His obituary says he was "Proud of his American Indian heritage." The movie was filmed four years after Abbott graduated from UT, so the period works.

169

But I can't find any mention of him being McQueen's bodyguard. That is unsurprising since Mark said McQueen "Had a habit of being rude to folks."

I met McQueen briefly at the movie's wrap party at Aquarena Springs Hotel in San Marcos, and he was very nice, but that was only a ten-minute encounter.

When I turned to walk down the Aquarena Springs Hotel stairs, he asked if he could walk with me. I never understood why, except perhaps my height, 6'5", and weight 220. Anyone approaching him would think I was his bodyguard. I'm sure that was wishful thinking, but I needed an answer to everything then. Life has a way of teaching you to get over yourself.

After further research through some of my friends, Tom Campbell and Billy Dale, who were freshmen during Danny Abbott's senior year. Tom said everyone called Danny "Chief." Tom and Billy would soon play on two of the three Texas Longhorns' national championship football teams.

☆   ☆   ☆

I never met Duke Carlisle, Steve Wooster, or Jay Cormier. But I did meet Darrell Royal. We became friends, not because of football, but because of music.

Coach Royal, Johnny Rodriguez, and I had breakfast at Cisco's Restaurant and Bakery in East Austin. At breakfast, I reminded Coach Royal that Coach Manley had recruited me, and Coach replied: "Remind me again, why didn't you play for us?"

170

When I told him I lacked the math courses, he said, "You'd be surprised how many others didn't play for us for that same reason."

He also asked me why I went to Southwest Texas State University (Texas State today). I responded with what I thought was a funny answer, "All the pretty girls."

Coach looked me straight in the eyes and said, "That's a hell of a reason." He paused, smiled, and added, "The University of Texas has pretty girls, too."

Years later, I asked Coach Royal a question I knew he wouldn't answer, "Who was the greatest player you ever coached?"

Coach instantly responded, Tommy Nobis. Coach Royal introduced me to Earl Campbell, who became my friend. Earl was at the top of almost everyone's list.

I miss those days. And I miss all my friends that are no longer with us. The Good News is I'll see them all again— at least, that is my prayer. And I might ask Coach Royal, are you sure about Tommy Nobis? That one is for you, Earl Campbell.

I later was told Coach felt that way because Nobis played both ways, guard and linebacker.

Earl Campbell, Randy Willis, Willie Nelson.
Luck, Texas

Earl and I are in my backyard in Austin doing a PSA
with the UT Cheerleaders for their calendar.

Southwest Texas State University
San Marcos, Texas 78666   AC512 245-2581

Graduate School

November 20, 1980

Randall L. Willis
P.O. Box 351
Wimberley, TX 78676

Dear Mr. Willis:

Congratulations! On the basis of our present regulations, you have been granted admission into our Graduate School for Spring, 1981.

As a graduate student at Southwest Texas State University, you are responsible for being familiar with and abiding by all regulations as published in the *Graduate Bulletin*. Concurrence must always be obtained from your departmental graduate adviser *and* the Dean of the Graduate School for deviations from your official degree outline or for any special consideration request.

This admission does not guarantee acceptance into your chosen field, but your application is being forwarded to your proposed major department for approval and drafting of a degree outline as follows:
   Proposed Graduate Major: Business Administration
   Proposed Graduate Minor(s): N/A

Please note that, according to the *Graduate Bulletin*, "All applicants are required to take the APTITUDE portion of the GRADUATE RECORD EXAMINATION. The results of this examination must be *received* in the Graduate Office *no later than the end of the first long semester* of the student's enrollment in the Graduate School." If you have not already taken the GRE, you need to arrange to do so at the *earliest* possible date this semester. You must have your official GRE score sent directly from the Educational Testing Service (Princeton, New Jersey) to our Graduate School.

Should you have any questions regarding our Graduate School, any of our staff members in the Graduate Office will be more than happy to assist you.

Sincerely,

Cheryl J. Morriss

Cheryl J. Morriss
Coordinator, Graduate Admissions
  and Records

(You'll need to take the GRE no later than February 7, 1981. The deadline date to mail the GRE application to the testing service is January 2, 1981).

cc: student's file (1)

(The GRE Aptitute Test is a composite of the Quantitative and Verbal portions only).
the progressive university with a proud past

Southwest Texas State University is an affirmative action, equal opportunity educational institution.

I was accepted into Graduate School in 1980 at Southwest Texas State University, where I attended for six years. I recommended the Master of Business Administration (MBA) degree to my son Aaron Willis. It would become his postgraduate degree, opening many doors for him.

173

CHAPTER 25
A VILLAGE CALLED WIMBERLEY
1972

When I arrived on campus in the Fall of 1968, there were bumper stickers on numerous cars that read, "Mickey Mouse wears a Jim McCrocklin watch."

A few months later, in April 1969, James McCrocklin resigned as university president. It had been revealed that significant sections of his 1954 doctoral thesis were plagiarized. One of my professors showed his thesis in our class on an overhead projector, showing how it had been plagiarized.

Some said people were out to get him because he was closely linked to President Lyndon Johnson. McCrocklin served as his Under Secretary of Health, Education, and Welfare from July 1968 to January 1969. I had no opinion because I was too busy keeping my head above water. I felt I was drowning in a sea of financial challenges.

McCrocklin went into the real estate business in Central Texas, living in Wimberley until he died in 1998. I bought my first purchase of land in Wimberley through him. He gave me great advice on buying and selling real estate. I found him among the most brilliant people I've ever known. I liked him. It taught me that one wrong choice can bring down everything you've built in your life. Today, his granddaughter is good friends with my children. The entire family is first class.

Later in the year, on November 13, 1969, ten students were suspended from Texas State for protesting the Vietnam War. I witnessed their protest as I walked to class. They became known as the "San Marcos 10." Perhaps I was wrong about my guilt for not serving in Vietnam, I thought. Look how brave these students are. They just lost their opportunity for a college degree and all the money they had spent thus far for one.

✮   ✮   ✮

I worked part-time in college, driving a truck hauling gasoline for Steve Gregg on Post Road in San Marcos. Mr. Gregg was a bulk agent for Humble Oil and Refining Company. The pay was $1.50 an hour. He explained that the City of San Marcos did not allow the sizeable 6,000-plus gallon tankers in downtown San Marcos for fear if one blew up, so would the city. He said this had happened in Luling years before.

I would drive a small tanker truck holding around 1,500 gallons to downtown gas stations, farmers, and private airstrips in cow pastures for crop dusters.

Mr. Gregg added that the best way not to have a wreck was not to get close to another vehicle. And if I did have a wreak, I was a dead man. He got my attention.

He never failed to mention he was thankful I was not one of those long-haired, marijuana-smoking hippies at Southwest Texas State University, where I was a student.

I assured him I was a redneck hayseed cowboy, which was easy to see. I failed to mention I had many friends in that other category.

One sunny day, Mr. Gregg said I need you to drive the truck to a small village called Wimberley, only 20 minutes away. He warned me of the steep decline to the town called

175

Spoke Hill. It was named because the wagon wheel spokes would break due to the strain of descending and ascending the hill before horseless carriages—aka automobiles.

As I descended Spoke Hill in my tanker, I saw a view of The Texas Hill Country for the first time. "Wow, we don't have anything like this on the Old Danbury Road," I thought.

Before I reached the bottom of the hill, I had decided to move to Wimberley when I graduated from college.

Esso Gas Station (Humble Dealer)
Wimberly Square Wimberley, Texas

Esso Station, located at Wimberley Square

I bought my first track of land on the Blanco River through the former President of Southwest Texas State, Jim McCrocklin, who was now a Real Estate Broker.   The two acres sold for $4,000. $400 down. $40 per month for ten years, 8% interest.

I knew I was a "Land Baron" when, a year later, someone offered me twice that amount, $8,000. Now, with my BBA (Bachelor of Business Administration) degree in hand, I knew it would never go much higher.   Later, as the prices

176

increased over ten times, it left an everlasting impression that education was "Monkey see—Monkey do"—not common sense.

I've told this story to my three sons and grandchildren many times, adding that they would not be living in Wimberley today nor met their wives, and more importantly, would my grandchildren ever been born if I'd not made that trip to gas up the Esso station on the Wimberley town square. My grandchildren finish the story for me these days, as my sons did.

The station is gone, but my memories remain. It's a restaurant today with folks drinking a glass of wine under the shade trees where I once labored in the hot Texas sun with holes in my shoes for mere pennies for my future family— never mind—that parts for only them.

The old Esso gas pumps were leaning against the left side of the building for many years after the station closed. I wish I had bought them to repeatedly point to them when I tell my family this story.

Perhaps the visual props would make the story more interesting the 500th time I tell it. Or maybe my sons bought them and will not tell me where they hid them.

Oh, by the way, kids, did I ever tell you what gas cost then? And how I walked backward, barefooted in the snow to school.

CHAPTER 26
BROTHER JB YOUNG
WIMBERLEY, TEXAS

The old preacher did not mince words when he spoke of the American flag at age 94 on the 4th of July at Wimberley First Baptist. He was known as Bro. Young by everyone.

Brother JB Young of Wimberley flew the first combat mission of World War II on the morning of December 7, 1941, from Hickam Field at Pearl Harbor after being grazed by a Japanese bullet.

He looked around to make sure no women or children could hear him when he said, "It grazed one of my nipples."

He got off the ground at Hickam Field with tape across his chest to find and destroy the Japanese Fleet. He added, "I'm sure glad I didn't locate them; I had no idea how many they were."

I first met Brother Young in 1974 when I transferred my membership by letter from Second Baptist in Angleton to First Baptist Wimberley. He was the pastor. I have never known a finer and more consistent Christian couple than Bro. and Mrs. Young. It has been a beautiful privilege from God to have been able to call them friends.

When Bro. Young was sent home from the war in the Pacific in 1943; he was one the most decorated soldiers in World War II. He had flown 66 missions, been awarded two Silver Stars, two Purple Hearts, two Flying Crosses, and four Air Medals, and received a Presidential Citation.

Of all the missions J.B. Young would attempt, none would surpass the one he began in 1940. On May 7 of that year, Bro. Young disembarked a converted cattle boat the navy used to transport troops to Hawaii. He was met by Rev. E.K. Begley, pastor of a little mission church named O'ahu Baptist Church.

One day, while visiting Begley's home, Bro. Young saw a church newspaper from Macedonia, Arkansas. What caught his eye was a picture of a pretty Christian girl in the paper singing in the choir.

Since Begley was from Macedonia, Bro. Young asked him: "Do you know this girl?"

"Sure," Begley said. "She is Arline Frank from Madeconia, why don't you write her?" Folks back home were encouraged to write soldiers.

This began a correspondence by mail that lasted until June 21, 1943, the day Bro. Young arrived in Macedonia to meet Arline face-to-face for the first time at 10 a.m. The next day, at 8 a.m., the two became husband and wife.

As they drove off for their honeymoon, Bro. Young overheard Arline's father say, "She'll return in a month. It will never last."

Bro. J.B. Young died on May 21, 2011, at 95. He and Mrs. Young are buried side by side in the Wimberley Cemetery. I visit their grave often when I get an inspection or oil change at Conley's. Their grave is a few feet across the road.

He was my Pastor, mentor, friend, fishing buddy, and surrogate father.

179

I asked him once if he believed in the inerrancy of the Bible. He responded, "I sure do. But suppose I didn't; which scriptures would I toss out? The ones that didn't agree with my sinful lifestyle or the ones I didn't understand. The later I accept by faith, the former will send you to hell."

He added that you should constantly ask yourself who the writer in the Bible is writing to, a lost person or a saved person. That advice has helped me through my journey in life.

This video of Bro. Young, at age 94, reciting "The Ragged Old Flag," by Johnny Cash, will bless your heart: http://youtu.be/n9Bem2Ej3Wq

This recitation was part of an Independence Day service held on July 4th, 2010, at First Baptist Church, Wimberley, Texas.

The following year, angels escorted him to his new home and face-to-face with his Lord, whom he had preached about for seven decades.

CHAPTER 27
STEEL GUITAR MAN

After World War II, my father played the lap steel guitar in Happy McNichol's band at the Wigwam dancehall and other venues.

The beer joint was located along the banks of an old mining pond in Forest Hill, Louisiana. Chicken wire fencing wrapped around the bandstand so the band would not get hit with beer bottles.

Daddy and his brother Herman Willis got into a brawl at the Wigwam once with five soldiers from nearby Camp Claiborne. That fight inspired the fight scene in my novel *Destiny*. Daddy had a rawhide toughness yet was respectful, charming, and kind-hearted—especially to children, women, veterans, and those older than him.

He would often say, "There are three things I can't stand: cold coffee, wet toilet paper, and a damn smart alec." The latter he did not abide, especially if he had been drinking.

Alcohol and Daddy did not mix well; he later got into another fight at another nearby bar, the Ranch House, three minutes away outside Camp Claiborne. There were also numerous pawn shops and "Cat Houses" near Camp Claiborne.

Daddy hopped onto the Ranch House's bar's counter when a bartender refused to serve him. As he walked down the bar, he kicked every beer bottle into the mirrored wall behind the bar. Daddy had worn out his welcome at that establishment. He never returned.

Daddy stopped drinking when his friend Happy McNichols told him to turn down his lap steel guitar amp on stage at the Wigwam. Daddy stood and slugged McNichols on stage in front of a packed house.

Daddy realized he had a problem, a severe problem. Hitting a close friend crossed a line. Once he starts courting Mother, there could be no hangovers, hangouts, or hangups. The drinking and bar fights were a thing of the past. Unfortunately, it also ended his steel guitar playing days except at home and an occasional home or barn dance.

One day, Daddy's stepdaughter and my half-sister Johnnie Ruth brought home her young beau, Jimmy Day, to meet our parents. Johnnie Ruth was 15 years older than me. Our home was located near Longleaf, Louisiana, within walking distance of the Ole Willis Home Place overlooking Barber Creek.

Daddy was practicing on his steel guitar when they arrived after school. Jimmy knew of Daddy's reputation on the steel guitar and with his fist. Jimmy asks Daddy to teach him to tune and play the steel guitar. Daddy did just that.

The Wigwam was the first venue where both Jimmy and Daddy played. Harold Whatley, from Longleaf, continued to teach Jimmy steel guitar licks.

Harold later wrote a big hit with Mel Tillis about the Longleaf Crowell and Spencer Sawmill, which was within walking distance of our home and entitled *Saw Mill*, released in 1959.

Jimmy's Dad worked at the sawmill's commissary and was later transferred from the Crowell and Spencer Sawmill in Longleaf to another mill.

After moving, Jimmy became best friends in high school with Floyd Cramer.

Having dinner one night at the Broken Spoke in Austin, Jimmy told me, over a chicken fried steak, that Floyd initially wanted him to teach him the steel guitar. Jimmy informed him, "I'm the steel player; choose another instrument."

Floyd decided on the piano. Jimmy also told me about working with Hank Williams Sr., Patsy Cline, and Elvis that night. I often hired Jimmy to back the recording artist I managed, but that story is for a future volume in my memoir.

In the beginning, Jimmy had considerable difficulty with his fretwork. His problems were solved in 1949 when he saw Shot Jackson providing steel support for the Bailes Brothers. Jackson influenced Jimmy's style greatly. They later became friends.

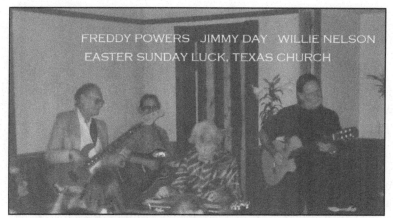

Easter Sunday at Willie's Luck, Texas Church.
It mainly was Gospel Music. No sermon.

Easter Sunday at Willie Nelson's Luck, Texas Church.
Aaron, Josh, and Adam Willis

☆　　☆　　☆

According to Jimmy, this date should have been 1955 at the Reo Palm Isle Longview, Texas.

The inscription reads, "To my lifelong friend, Randy." Jimmy Day

Jimmy Day soon began working with Webb Pierce, whom he recorded on his first sessions. He introduced Web Pierce to Floyd Kramer.

185

They both played on Pierce's number one hit, *This Heart Belongs,* just before Jimmy's 18th birthday.

In the spring of 1952, Jimmy began a six-month stint backing Hank Williams Sr. In November, less than two months before Hank's tragic death, he asked Jimmy to join a new band he planned to assemble the following year. That tour never happened due to Hank's death on New Year's Day, 1953.

With the advent of the pedal steel guitar in 1954, Jimmy began moving away from the lap steel guitar during a tenure with Lefty Frizzell and his final gig playing the steel guitar at the Louisiana Hayride, backing Elvis Presley.

Jimmy told me that Elvis asked him to play the steel guitar in his new band. Jimmy told him his dream was to go to Nashville, so he declined.

He added, "If I'd said yes, there might be a steel guitar in rock and roll today."

Jimmy became known as "Mr. Country Soul" with his legendary Blue Darlin' steel guitar.

Floyd Cramer wrote and performed his mega-hit *Last Date* in 1960. It sold over a million copies. Floyd became known for his "slip note" piano style, in which an out-of-key note slides into the correct note.

Few musicians are so highly regarded that their names become synonymous with their instruments. Floyd Cramer and Jimmy Day are two of them.

I thought of Jimmy the other day, listening to the radio, when I heard his opening licks of Ray Price's *Crazy Arms*.

Jimmy and Floyd toured with Elvis in his band before he became famous.

It was Cramer's piano playing on Elvis Presley's first RCA Victor single, *Heartbreak Hotel*. Jimmy was in the studio as a guest of Floyd's but did not play on the record.

Jimmy played the steel guitar for Web Pierce, Hank Williams Sr., Elvis, Patsy Cline, Ray Price, Jim Reeves, Johnny Horton, Willie Nelson, and many others.

After the Wigwam became the Lake Shamaree bar, Willie Nelson and George Jones played at Jimmy's suggestion.

Randy Willis and Jimmy Day front right

187

Benny McArthur (with George Strait's band), Jimmy Day, Randy Willis, and Craig Dillingham (Tanya Tucker's boyfriend). I had hired them to back a recording artist.

188

Marty Stuart, Randy Willis, and Jimmy Day

Adam, Josh, and Aaron Willis with Jimmy Day.

189

CHAPTER 28
BIG JAKE

In my novels *Louisiana Wind, Texas Wind, and Destiny*, Julian "Jake" Willis is Boss Man Jake.

Few years would impact my life more than 1919 did.

In 1919, the third and final wave of the influenza pandemic occurred. The pandemic killed 675,000 people in the United States. That number included family members.

In 1919, President Wilson signed a proclamation commemorating the end of fighting in World War I as Armistice Day. My cousins and great-uncles returned home from the Great War.

1919, the Eighteenth Amendment was ratified, authorizing the prohibition of alcoholic beverages. It did not stop my namesake and Grandfather, Randall Lee "Rand" Willis. He would hide from my grandmother on Barber Creek and drink high-proof distilled spirits called moonshine.

In 1919, Congress approved the 19th Amendment to legalize women's suffrage. The following year, my seven-year-old future mother, Ruth Lawson Willis, received the right to vote when she came of age.

In 1919, Norman Saurage discovered the secret of making my favorite coffee in the home of LSU, Baton Rouge. He named it Community Coffee. I call Community Coffee my "drug dealer." I lived in Baton Rouge near LSU's campus on Belmont Avenue for three years, attended the games, sat in "Death Valley," and became a fan. Geaux Tigers!

In 1919, Arnold Rothstein deliberately paid members of the Chicago White Sox to lose the World Series. Babe Ruth said Shoeless Joe Jackson was "The greatest hitter I'd ever seen." Shoeless Joe admitted that he cheated. The quote, "Say it ain't so, Joe," became famous.

In 1919, my favorite baseball sports hero, Jackie Robinson, was born. He was an American professional baseball player who became the first African American to play in the Major League.

And in 1919, my all-time hero, my father, Julian "Jake" Willis, was born.

> "Gatsby hesitated, then added cooly: He's the man who fixed the World Series back in 1919."
> —F. Scott Fitzgerald's *The Great Gatsby*

Randy Willis standing behind the '39 Lincoln door.

My two-year-old granddaughter Juliette Willis was named after my Dad Julian Willis. I taught her how to neck rein on this day in 2024, not long before her 3rd birthday, like Daddy taught me. She rode again a couple days later. When I told her it was getting too cold, she said I don't care. Juliette's French origin meaning is "little Julia." Julian, my father's name, is a male version of Juliette.

CHAPTER 29
ENCHANTING WOMAN
ENCHANTING ROCK

I arose on a cold morning at 5:30 on March 15, 1986, at our deer lease owned by EJ Moss between Llano and Fredericksburg at the intersection of Texas Highway 16 and Ranch Road 965. There is a Jack C. Hays Historical Marker there today.

Our leased part of the large Moss Ranch was in the back section, overshadowed by the foothills of Loneman Mountain facing Enchanted Rock. The view rivals Devil's Backbone near Wimberley. Daddy and I were the only two there that day. That is the only time I can remember that ever occurring.

Daddy opened his travel trailer door before sunrise as I threw a pound of bacon into our cast iron skillet near our campfire. He had sweat on his brow and looked haggard.

Morning "Rand," he said. A name he seldom called me.

"You look tired," I said.

"Didn't sleep a wink," he yawned.

I pointed to a pot of boiling coffee on the campfire. "It's darker than midnight under a skillet," I said, knowing that's what Daddy preferred.

I never was one to pry with him. "Do you know what day it is?" He sat next to the campfire and looked puzzled. "My namesake and your Daddy would have been 100 today. That sparked something in him that I had never seen and never did again.

"Sometimes, I can't sleep when I think of that damn war." He began to open up about the loss of his first cousin and dear friend, Bobby Willis, on the USS Arizona at Pearl Harbor on December 7, 1941, the loss of his squad after basic training in a plane crash. He was not on the plane because he was in the hospital with yellow jaundice. Why was he spared? He spoke of what he had seen and done on Iwo Jima. It was the first and last time he ever mentioned those details.

"What a sacrifice," I said.

"It was my duty. The ones who sacrificed never made it back. They were the heroes, not me."

But then, he looked down and said under his breath, "Dorene was the hardest." He stood and added, "It's getting late; let's head up Loneman Mountain and build that deer blind." As we climbed into his old 4-wheel drive Ford pickup, he mumbled, "Damn, Preacher." I had no clue what he meant, nor was I about to ask.

He carried five personal items as he climbed Mount Suribachi on Iwo Jima:

1) His dog tags to identify him if he was killed in action.
2) A bracelet with an inscription from his wife.
3) A photo of his mother with him and his two brothers when they were little boys.
4) A newspaper headline entitled *First Alexandria Casualty in War* about his first cousin Bobby Willis.
5) The New Testament included a strong exhortation from President Franklin D. Roosevelt.

194

All five had a profound effect on his life. All five are in my possession.

Julian Willis is in the center. World War II

✮   ✮   ✮

Julian Willis standing on the wing. World War II

His dog tags to identify him if he was (KIA)
killed in action.

A bracelet with an inscription from his wife, Dorene.

My Grandmother Lillie Gertrude Hanks Willis with her three sons: Howard Willis (1915-1993), Herman Willis (1918-1977), and my dad Julian Willis (1919-1995). circa 1922

A photo of his mother with him and his two brothers, Howard and Herman Willis, when they were little boys.

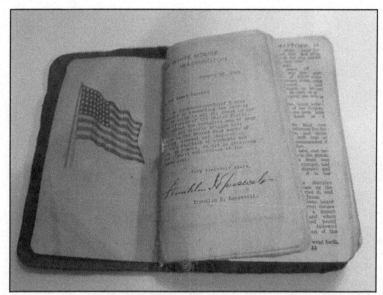

Daddy's New Testament included a strong exhortation from
President Franklin D. Roosevelt.

"To the Armed Forces:

"As Commander-in-Chief," he wrote, "I take pleasure in
commending the reading of the Bible to all who serve in the
armed forces on the United States. It is a fountain of
strength."

My father kept this Bible's well-worn pages for 54 years
until he died in 1995.

☆   ☆   ☆

First Alexandria
Casualty in War

Robert (Bobby) K. Willis, 19, above, son of R. K. Willis of Alexandria, has been reported missing at Pearl Harbor. He is the first local boy to be listed as a casualty since the United States entered the w...

A newspaper headline entitled First Alexandria Casualty in War about Daddy, Julian Willis's first cousin Bobby Willis.

199

Daddy's father and my namesake, Randall Lee "Rand" Willis, died May 14, 1940, of stomach cancer at age 54 caused by his addiction to alcohol.

Daddy was 20 when his father died, and he joined the Civilian Conservation Corps (CCC), a voluntary government work relief program. The CCC provided him shelter, clothing, food, and a wage of $30 per month, of which $25 must be sent home per the CCC. Daddy was sent to the Pacific Northwest CCC Rujada Forest Camp, which is dedicated to forestry and conservation projects. The forest was not the only draw; the use of horses in the mountains was a perfect fit.

Daddy's first cousin, Robert "Kenneth "Bobby" Willis Jr, enlisted in the Navy on July 31, 1940. Bobby worked as a part-time librarian at a public school in the spring of 1940, earning far less than the CCC paid Daddy. Bobby encouraged Daddy to join the military and make something of himself in service of his country. It was the same advice Bobby's father had given him, leading to him joining the Navy.

Daddy, Julian Willis, at Rujada Forest Camp in Oregon
Civilian Conservation Corps (CCC)

Daddy, Julian Willis, at Rujada Forest Camp in Oregon.
Civilian Conservation Corps (CCC)

Daddy, Julian Willis, at Rujada Forest Camp in Oregon.
Civilian Conservation Corps (CCC)

Daddy's first cousin, Robert "Kenneth "Bobby" Willis Jr., was entombed at the bottom of Pearl Harbor on December 7, 1941.

Unemployment was near 15% in 1940 despite Franklin Roosevelt's assertion in his Inaugural Address seven years before, "The only thing we have to fear is fear itself."

Daddy joined the US Army Air Corps (#4 152 091) at Camp Shelby, Mississippi, on October 14, 1941.

In only 54 days, his training progressed to an accelerated fast track when the Japanese attacked Pearl Harbor on December 7, 1941.

Two weeks later, Daddy received confirmation his first cousin and dear friend Robert Kenneth "Bobby" Willis Jr. was KIA on the USS Arizona. Bobby Willis is still entombed at the bottom of Pearl Harbor.

Bobby was the first casualty from Rapides Parish, Louisiana, in World War II.

After the news of Bobby's death, the war became personal–very personal to Daddy.

It was the first in a series of wartime events to mold Daddy's character and sometimes harden his heart.

Daddy was stationed at Keesler Field in Biloxi, Mississippi, for basic training when the Japanese attacked Pearl Harbor.

The next day, President Franklin Roosevelt requested a Declaration of War.

"Mr. Vice President, and Mr. Speaker, and Members of the Senate and House of Representatives.

"Yesterday, December 7, 1941—a date which will live in infamy—the United States of America was suddenly and deliberately attacked by naval and air forces of the Empire of Japan...

"No matter how long it may take us to overcome this premeditated invasion, the American people in their righteous might will win through to absolute victory.

203

"I believe that I interpret the will of the Congress and of the people when I assert that we will not only defend ourselves to the uttermost but will make it very certain that this form of treachery shall never again endanger us….

"I ask that the Congress declare that since the unprovoked and dastardly attack by Japan on Sunday, December 7, 1941, a state of war has existed between the United States and the Japanese empire."

☆   ☆   ☆

Keesler Field was activated only months before, in June. It had high-quality technical schools. Daddy's fellow recruits became his close friends.

When the time came for them to fly out, Daddy was devastated when he could not fly with them because he had yellow jaundice.

While in the hospital, the news came that their plane had crashed. There were no survivors.

Daddy received a New Testament at Keesler Field. All Christians received a pocket-sized volume of the New Testament and the Book of Psalms.

The New Testament includes a strong appeal from President Franklin D. Roosevelt.

January 25, 1941
To the Armed Forces:

"As Commander-in-Chief I take pleasure in commending the reading of the Bible to all who serve in the armed forces of the United States. Throughout the centuries men of many faiths and diverse origins have found in the Sacred Book words of wisdom, counsel and inspiration. It is a foundation of strength and now, as always, an aid In attaining the highest aspirations of the human soul."

Very sincerely yours,
Franklin D. Roosevelt

Daddy finished basic training at Keesler Field on August 8, 1942. On August 15, 1942, he arrived at Hunter Army Airfield in Savannah, Georgia, as a member of the 302 Bombardment Squadron, 84th Bombardment Group, one of the first dive bomber units in the United States Army Air Corps. He was made Corporal.

Daddy finished basic training at Keesler Field on
August 8, 1942

He transferred to Drew Field in Tampa, Florida, on
January 8, 1943. On March 23, 1942, he joined the 407th
Bombardment Group (Dive). The air echelon was attached to
the Eleventh Air Force in Amchitka, Alaska.

Daddy performed combat operations against the
Japanese in the Aleutian Islands in the summer of 1943. He
told me they lost more pilots and planes to the weather than
they did to the Japanese.

After combat in the Aleutian Islands, he transferred to Woodward, Oklahoma. The United States Army Air Forces built the airfield in the fall of 1942 and early 1943 as an aircrew training field. He was made Staff Sergeant on June 8, 1943.

The facility opened in March 1943 during World War II and was known as Woodward Army Airfield. The airfield was a considerable employer for the sparsely polluted area near the Northeastern corner of the Texas Panhandle.

It would be here Daddy would make a decision that would trouble him for the rest of his life. He met a young woman, beautiful. She was from the neighboring county of Ellis, on the Texas Panhandle's border. Ellis County only had a couple thousand people. Her parents own horses, and she loved horses like Daddy.

JULIAN "JAKE" WILLIS & DORENE RICHARDSON WILLIS
AUGUST, 1944 ELLIS COUNTY OKLAHOMA

Daddy and his wife, Dorene Richardson. They married on August 6, 1944, in Ellis County, Oklahoma.

He knew his days were numbered stateside as the war raged in the Pacific. On August 6, 1944, they were married. Little did he know he would soon fly out to one of the most dangerous places on earth, Iwo Jima, by way of Guam and Hawaii.

On Daddy's flight overseas, the plane stopped over on the island of Guam to refuel and for the soldiers to rest and eat. Americans had recaptured the Japanese-held island of Guam in the summer of 1944.

As Daddy departed the plane, a roster of soldiers was taken. When Daddy gave his name, the man making the list said the aircraft that had just landed also had a Willis on it named Herman. As Daddy entered the mess hall, his brother Herman Willis shouted and ran toward him. Neither were raised to be overly affectionate. But, they were on this day.

They briefly visited for a couple of hours in the vast Western Pacific. As Herman stood to board his plane, he asked Daddy, "Did you get a Christmas gift from Mama? I received mine a few days ago." That would also be discussed around the campfire at our dear lease.

With the recent death of his father, headed to an unknown land during Christmas, the gift from his mother would be extra special this year. And he had his beautiful new bride waiting for him back home.

Although Daddy and Dorene's romance was a May-December type, they were both young and in love. Daddy was lonely as Christmas approached. The reunion with Herman was an ointment for his soul.

During that time, Daddy and Dorene wrote many love letters. He had all his military pay and savings sent directly to her so they would have a nest egg if and when he returned from overseas.

When the war ended in 1945, he sailed to San Diego from Iwo Jima.

After arriving in San Diego, he still had to go home to Longleaf, Louisiana, after rendezvousing with his wife. The reunion was all set by mail. Daddy was beside himself with anticipation. The military had done its part. The rest of the journey was his responsibility.

In San Diego, he bought a used Harley-Davidson motorcycle and headed straight to his reunion with his sweetheart.

Julian Willis San Diego
When he arrived, she was gone. He never saw her again.

After Daddy died in 1995, I found the bracelet she gave him before leaving for the Pacific in a coin purse. The bracelet read, "HAND OFF. HE'S ALL MINE DORENE." His military dog tags, a ring with JW stenciled, and an Army Aviation pin were also in the coin pouch. Daddy kept the bracelet from Dorene until he died 51 years later.

It was all in a larger box with their marriage license, with her name, Dorene Richardson. Military discharge papers, the New Testament, a photo of his mother with his two brothers as boys, and a diary entitled "U.S. Army Snapshots." With essential dates and events during the war.

That diary and other documents are my primary source for much of this, along with my visits with Uncle Herman and Daddy during our visit to the deer lease in 1986.

During World War II, United States military restrictions prohibited American servicemen from keeping personal journals. He must have written the later part after the end of the war.

Daddy would engage the Japanese in combat on Iwo Jima. Iwo Jima's Battle lasted from February 19 to March 26, 1945. The photos Daddy took on Iwo Jima included slain Japanese soldiers. They are too gruesome to share. Iwo Jima was declared "secured," but it wasn't.

The enemies were hidden in caves. That's where my father encountered and fought them after the US Army Air Corps arrived.

Daddy's brother, Herman Willis, was in Okinawa. On April 1, 1945, the initial invasion of Okinawa was the most massive amphibious assault in the Pacific Theater of War II.

There were approximately 160,000 casualties on both sides. The cost of freedom continued to climb.

Daddy and his brother Herman were sure to engage the Japanese again, but it would be on Japanese soil the next time.

The US Army Air Corps (today's Air Force) needed the island of Iwo Jima as an emergency landing site for its B-29 Superfortress strategic bombing campaign against the Empire of Japan.

Based upon the fierce Japanese resistance encountered in the island fighting, one US government estimate predicted the war would last another year and a half. Another expert had the ultimate cost of the invasion of Japan as 1.7 to 4 million lives.

One-third of all marines killed during WW II had already died on Iwo Jima. The chance of being killed in the invasion was high.

President Harry Truman ended those plans by having two nuclear weapons dropped over the Japanese cities of Hiroshima and Nagasaki on August 6 and 9, 1945, respectively.

That decision may have saved my father's and his brother's lives.

Daddy climbed Mount Suribachi while on Iwo Jima. He taught me how to climb mountains too! In my mind, the Bible and the bracelet represented his hope for the future. His climb up Mount Suribachi was a victory over extreme adversity.

Daddy became a Technical Sergeant in the 52nd Air Engineer Squadron, 330th Air Services Group. He was honorably discharged in Ft Bliss, Texas, on November 22, 1945. He stood 5' 11 ½" and weighed 146 pounds soaking wet, according to his discharge papers.

Julian "Jake" Willis atop Mount Suribachi
after the Battle of Iwo Jima (February 19-March 26, 1945) in World War II.

Daddy atop Mount Suribachi while on Iwo Jima.

The emaciated soldier would find solace in his childhood home, the Ole Willis Home Place, and the hot meals his mother, Lillie, would cook.

The healing of a broken heart would take much, much, much longer. Perhaps a lifetime.

As mentioned before, The bracelet was inscribed, "HANDS OFF HE'S ALL MINE" DORENE." The irony was not lost on me.

He never found out why she left him or where she went, but I did years later. Three years after Daddy died in 1995, a new company named Google came online.

With my Sherlock Holmes determination and Google's search engine, I located Dorene's daughter through inquiries on ancestor.com. Dorene's hometown and last name were on their marriage license. Dorene's daughter was gracious and understanding.

Julian Willis World War II

When I complained to my eldest son Aaron when he got a small tattoo on his back, he responded, "Grandpa has one." Daddy's entire United States Army Air Corps squadron got the same tattoo. It read "Keep'Em Flying" with "Flyer" underneath. Many of those men died with that slogan inked on theirs arms in World War II.

One dare not ever have an issue with Daddy's tattoo. Although, they are the only two in our family to date.

Julian Willis World War II

I emailed her photos I thought might be her mother I found in my Dad's old box of belongings. Her mother had told her briefly of Daddy. I also wanted to know if I had an unknown half-sibling.

While Daddy was overseas, her mother, Dorene, met another soldier. During that time, she continued to receive Daddy's military pay.

Daddy had no clue she wasn't home waiting for him. I wished Daddy had been alive when I discovered all this to have given him some closure.

Dorene never sent a "Dear John" letter, postcard, telegram, carrier pigeon, or smoke signal to Daddy.

My Grandmother told me she could hear him weeping in the middle of the night after returning home from overseas.

I discovered her complete name was Ella Dorene Richardson online. She was born on April 19, 1928, and died on August 16, 1974. During the mid-1960s, Daddy, Mama, my sister, and I stopped at Dorene's mother's home in Oklahoma on our way to Yellowstone National Park. None of us knew in advance why Daddy's detoured.

Daddy stopped again in the mid-1970s on his way to the Calgary Stampede Rodeo in Canada with his new wife, Marie. Both times, her mother was vague about where she was. Daddy was seeking the answer to that age-old question of why. And perhaps she has an unknown child by him. Daddy never knew she died in 1974.

It is interesting to note Marie looked a lot like Dorene. Sometimes, it's hard to let go of your first love, and as the Good Book says, "forget the things of the past."

Remember when Uncle Herman asked in Guam if a Christmas gift was mailed to Daddy by Grandma? After Daddy and I built the deer blind on the EJ Moss Ranch on

March 15, 1986, I assumed Daddy had finished pouring out his heart.

That is until he brought up that gift. He told me he never received the gift. It was clear he was still upset after 41 years. I knew he had difficulty forgetting what he perceived as wrong, but this was ridiculous. No, I did not share that thought with him.

I listened but later thought it was in the middle of a war; who cares about a gift? It was probably lost anyway. Uncle Herman was 11 months older than Daddy. They were best friends as close as possible, but what my grandmother told me of their sibling rivalry became clear to me that night around a campfire.

It also occurred to me that perhaps Uncle Herman never received a Christmas gift but wondered if Daddy had. Neither Daddy nor Uncle Herman would have dared ask their mother about that.

Grandma might not have mailed any Christmas gifts that year because the war was raging, rationing was in full swing, and soldiers were forbidden from writing details of their troop's movements.

It was a lesson to me as those great theologians and soothsayers The Eagles once sang, *Get Over It*. When they're fretting, I have told my family, "Life's short; don't major in the minor things. And when you can eat dessert first."

CHAPTER 30
I WANT NO PART
IF THAT'S CHRISTIANITY

Daddy would soon join the church for solace near his childhood home, The Ole Willis Home Place, near Longleaf, Louisiana. Daddy became best friends with the Pastor.

One day, while they fished Cocodrie Lake, the preacher confided in him that he would occasionally slip off for a *rendezvous* with a woman who was also a church member. He even bragged about it.

Like Dorene, the pastor was in an adulterous affair. My father never attended another church except for weddings and funerals, that is, until three years later when he asked a woman living a half mile down Willis-Gunter Road from the Ole Willis Home Place for a date.

She was a widow, six years older than him, with four children. He had known her all his life. He had known her late husband, too, whom she married when Daddy was only 14.

She accepted, provided they attended church and dinner on the grounds after church at Longleaf Baptist Church the following Sunday. She was my future Mother, his Mother's dearest friend, and the best woman I ever knew.

Daddy still believed in Christ but did not trust organized religion. His church would be in a deer blind on the side of Loneman Mountain facing Enchanted Rock. He would advise me, tell beautiful stories, and pour me a plastic glass of blackberry wine in that sanctuary. I considered it the Lord's Supper. Hopefully, the Good Lord was not offended.

217

My grandson Corbin Willis atop Enchanted Rock with his great-grandfather Jake Willis's old dear lease in the background at the foot of Loneman Mountain.

218

December, 1984. Jake Willis is about to show his grandsons, Adam, age 2, and Aaron, age 7, how to shoot.

Aaron, Adam (Corbin's Dad), Daddy, and
Josh Willis near Llano, Texas

Adam, Aaron, and Daddy. Loneman Mountain.

Until the day Daddy died when the American flag passed by at a rodeo or any other event, Daddy stood, took off his cowboy hat, and placed his right hand over his heart. He would often bow his head and give thanks. The Star-Spangled Banner received the same respect.

Daddy was Trail Boss for nine years of the Brazoria County Trail Ride. He was a lifetime member of the Brazoria County Fair and Rodeo Association and a board member. He was a Brazoria County Cattleman's Association member and the Brazoria County 100 Club.

Jake Willis Angleton Youth Rodeo 1989

He loved teaching kids to ride horses and enjoyed seeing their excitement when they learned to enjoy them.

He had more friends than anyone I've ever known.

Randy Willis and Jake Willis: The days when
Daddy training "Paint" a wild Mustang to pray.

Daddy was diagnosed with prostate cancer. I prayed for months, stood on every promise I could find in the Scriptures, pleaded the blood of Christ, got prayer chains going, fasted, and made promises to the Lord no one could have kept. Nothing works as cancer spreads throughout his worn-out body.

Soon, I got the dreaded call from his girlfriend while at MD Anderson Cancer Center in Houston. The doctors said he had less than a week to live. She added that Daddy noted I must head to Angleton tomorrow if I ever wanted to see him again. Daddy insisted on dying at home. That surprised no one.

The following morning, I headed from Wimberley to Angleton. I did okay until I got between Damon and Angleton near West Columbia and broke down weeping like a baby. I spoke not a word, just cried when a still, small voice that was as real to me as if the one speaking was seated next to me. "Why are you crying? He will not die." That was all that was said, not a syllable more.

There was no need for the Holy Spirit to repeat it as the most overwhelming peace I had ever known engulfed me. Within 30 minutes, I knocked on Daddy's front door. His girlfriend let me in, and I rushed into his room to share the good news.

He said, "Everyone wants to hope, but I'm afraid it's too late for that." We visited for a while. He gave me instructions concerning his funeral. I did not wish to argue the issue since he was frail.

As I left his room, his girlfriend motioned me to the kitchen and said, " I heard what you told him. I sit in the amen corner at church just like you do. You don't live down here.

He's getting worse every minute of every hour every day. You should not have given him a false hope. You're not the one having to watch him die; I am!"

I told her, I'm glad you feel that way because when he saddles and mounts his quarter horse again, you will know the power of the Lord Jesus Christ." She smirked, and I left to visit my brother Jerry.

A week passed, then two, then a month, when they returned to MD Anderson in Houston. When the test results came in, Daddy's Oncologists said, "I don't understand; all your tests are negative for cancer."

Several years later, I got an urgent page from Daddy. "Rand, I'm afraid this cancer has come back," he said.

"That's impossible. Jesus never healed imperfectly; you're going to die one day, but it will not be from cancer."

"Are you sure," he said.

"Just as sure as I am of this payphone booth, I'm standing inside, about to freeze to death."

Daddy died five years later when his heart gave out.

CHAPTER 31
SHOT DOWN IN MAY

This series of events changed my life.

In 1986, I divorced. On a business trip, I met a lady in Corpus Christi two years later.

We were both staying at the Holiday Inn on Corpus Christi Bay. I was in Corpus Christi as one of three board members appointed to the Texas Apartment Association Board by The Austin Apartment Association for a quarterly board meeting.

She was in Corpus Christi to recover from a divorce in Houston. We met in the sauna next to the indoor swimming pool.

She looked like Kate Beckinsale does today. After making small talk for 20 minutes and taking all the heat I could stand in the sauna, we moved to a table by the pool. I knew it was now or never, so I asked if she would like to have dinner with me.

She replied, "It's too soon, but I will meet you for coffee early tonight in the hotel lobby." We talked until midnight.

After my board meeting the next day, we drove to Mustang Island and Port A to see the sights and visit a friend from high school, Joel "Joe" Montgomery, who was in the area.

We went our separate ways but kept in touch by phone. We soon discovered we had much in common, including golf. I invited her to fly into Austin and play with me at the Austin Apartment Association's annual golf tournament. She was a much better golfer than me—which is not saying much.

As our romance intensified, we decided she should move to Austin. I rented a house for her, and she began to help me with my business ventures.

We realized our love was not a passing fancy, so we got engaged, but not all was well. When I first met her, I noticed she was thin. I also noticed she barely ate anything on her plate—just a few small bites.

☆   ☆   ☆

On New Year's Day, 1989, we watched a movie premiere on TV entitled *The Karen Carpenter Story*. As the movie progressed, she began to cry, saying repeatedly, "That's me."

I knew nothing about anorexia. Karen Carpenter died in 1983. Her death was attributed to heart failure because of anorexia nervosa. There was no social media then to sound the alarm. *The Karen Carpenter Story* did that.

Public awareness of anorexia nervosa and other eating disorders was transformed by Karen Carpenter's death and later movie. The sympathetic reporting of her illness prompted other celebrities to step forward and share their experiences.

It was an eating disorder that many would not acknowledge in those days. That may be true today, too.

We soon got an appointment with Dr. George Willeford, Jr. at St. David's Hospital. He was a wonderful, kind-hearted man. But he did not gloss over how she was putting herself in harm's way.

He explained that anorexia can rob your organs of nutrients and damage them even if you start eating correctly. The damage may have already been done.

She gained 10 pounds and seemed to be healthier. She died of a heart attack two months later.

✫   ✫   ✫

I fell apart and lost 30 pounds in 30 days. I blamed God and could not function. Within six months, I filed for bankruptcy in Chapter 7. I cried out to Christ, "Lord, where are you?"

I could not understand how a Christian girl and someone so young and kind could die. I'd go to the Scriptures to try and find answers. The first verse the Lord led me to change my life forever, "He who finds his life will lose it, and he who loses his life for My sake will find it." (Matthew 10:39)

That seemed simple enough; whoever finds his life will lose it. Okay, Randy, life is not about finding, acquiring, and accumulating things like sex, drugs, rock and roll. But that's not what it says.

"What have I been seeking?" I asked myself. I wrote down a list on a yellow tablet: success, education, health, wealth, social status, entertainment, pleasure, friends, family, children, and even religion. These are the things I've focused on. "Surely they are not all bad?"

227

But the scripture did not end there; what about the part that reads, "He who loses his life for My sake will find it."

I'm a little slow sometimes, "So Lord, life is not in the getting but in the giving?" I surmised.

He then led me to, "But seek first the kingdom of God and His righteousness, and all these things shall be added to you." (Matthew 6:33)

Now, that began to make sense, "I've spent all these years seeking and acquiring and still do not have the joy and peace You spoke of, Lord."

Even your universe is that way; the sun gives to the grass, the grass gives to the cow, and the cow gives me milk, and my part is to feed the cow. I don't pretend to know how the cow gives me white milk, but I reckon that part is called faith.

☆   ☆   ☆

That made me want to know Him. I read Jeremiah 29:13, which offers a powerful promise from God: When we earnestly seek Him wholeheartedly, we will find Him.

"Lord, how do I do that?" The most fervent of your apostles, Peter, denied you. Another betrayed you after seeing your miracles, and the others, save one, fled like a cat on a hot tin roof when you hung on a tree.

Nicodemus, the most pious of religious leaders, couldn't understand. The supreme religious body, the Sanhedrin, with Pharisees and Sadducees, didn't have a clue, although it was within their grasp in the books they held as truth.

The most radical of the spiritual, the Zealots, zeal misguided them. The most influential political leaders on earth could not see past themselves.

What hope is there for me to know You? You, Lord Jesus, are the Lord of Creation who spoke the Universe into existence. Who can dare get your attention?

I found the answer in Scripture. Jesus, leaving Jericho with His disciples, was joined by a great multitude. A blind man sat begging along the roadside. His name was Bartimaeus. When he discovered the clamor was about Jesus, he cried, "Jesus, Son of David, have mercy on me." When the crowd warned him to be quiet, he cried louder.

When Jesus heard him, the Bible says, "Jesus stood still." What does it take to get Jesus' attention? What does it take to stop God in the flesh, the Lord of Creation, in His tracks? The cry of a blind beggar.

Christ promised paradise with Him that day to a lowly thief on the cross. Jesus hears the cry of a baby. He takes our tears and puts them in a bottle. He attends the funeral of every sparrow. Our hairs are not counted, but each has a number. Where am I getting that from, the Bible.

Reach out to the last, the least, and the lost in His name and know His kindness, gentleness, goodness, love, peace, mercy, and grace. And you will know Him.

I started Operation Warm Heart, which feeds and clothes the needy of Central Texas. I became a volunteer at Children's Hospital in Austin. I began to work with a missionary in East Africa.

At this point, I'm supposed to write, "I became healthy and wealthy." That's not what happened.

Instead, I contracted tuberculosis from feeding the homeless, and my finances became so bad that I was near homelessness.

I read the Word of God, prayed, and watched the televangelist on TV who had all the answers. Many claimed to have Ph.D's. All I had to do was "plant a seed" by seeding them money. If I sent enough money, Jesus would give me a Pink Cadilac. They're confusing Jesus with Elvis. I call that the "doctrine" of "How To Drive to Hell in a Better Chevrolet."

As time crept by, I became oppressed and depressed to the point where I could not pray anymore. I gave up.

In my despair, I figured that the Lord either was not hearing my prayers or had chosen not to answer them. Why would He care about someone like me who had screwed up everything He had given me?

I was wasting my time asking Him for anything, I surmised. He's not a divine ATM. He hears the prayers of the righteous, and thousands in Austin are way more virtuous than me.

His words would not leave me alone, "He who finds his life will lose it, and he who loses his life for My sake will find it."

In my despair, I wrote in my Bible, "Lord Jesus, I'm broke, alone, and sick, but I agape you. All I have left is my salvation and my three sons. If you slay my three sons tonight and cast my soul into hell, I will still praise your Holy name."

His Glory filled my room. I do not have the words to explain what that means, but from then to this day, Christ is as real to me as the skin on my bones.

I know the Lord is never late, but I discovered He's never early. That's what is difficult. That is when you have to walk by faith. Everything changed that night, although I had no idea at the time. During my next visit to the doctor, I discovered the tuberculosis had vanished.

I thought of Christ feeding the 5,000 plus. He met their physical needs before meeting their spiritual needs. "But, Lord, I have no power to multiply five loaves of bread and two fish," I informed Him as if He didn't know.

I was right, but I would not be the One doing the multiplying. How easy it was for me to overlook that. It is a flaw in me to this very day. I somehow begin to gradually believe it's all about my self-effort, my dreams, my goals, and my plans; no, it's all about Him and His plans. He's an excellent multiplier. He's the only real source of life, peace, purpose, and joy.

I realized I was at ground zero with nothing to give. I asked my church, Hyde Park Baptist if they had any lost and found Bibles over the years. They had hundreds.

I took the Bibles to near the corner of East 8th and Red River, next to the Salvation Army in Austin, where many needy lived on a slab with no furniture inside the Salvation Army. I parked and sat on the tailgate of my pickup. A few people stopped, and I gave them a used Bible. I asked the Lord what his plans were next. There was no answer.

231

But I held to for some unexplained reason: "He who finds his life will lose it, and he who loses his life for My sake will find it." I didn't realize He had already given me the answer in that Scripture. There was no bolt of lightning, dream, or angel appearing. The answer was in the Word of God, not a feeling, although I felt I had so little to give.

When the first cold front blew in, I thought, Lord, these people need coats, and I only have one for this type of weather.

Unknowns to me, The Austin American Statesman photojournalist Ralph Barrera was across the street taking photos of me in the freezing weather. He later walked over and asked for my phone number. That's all he said. In a few days, one of those photos was on the front page of the City and State Section of the Austin American Statesman.

KIND HEARTS, WARM BODIES

Drive's sponsors collect winter clothing for the homeless

The photo was of me giving my coat to a homeless man. The man asked, "Mister, can I have your cost." I hesitated for a moment because I was wearing my expensive ski jacket. It still had old lift tickets attached from years before.

Ralph Barrera called me and asked if I'd like the newspaper plate on which the article was printed. He said

233

they had hundreds of inquiries. People wanted to donate coats.

The Austin American Statesman printed this article on November 14, 1991.

A few days later, a TV journalist named Keith Elkins arrived with television cameras. Then, every local station in Austin came to film me on the streets of Austin.

Keith Elkins was the first to do so when a woman with two small children asked me if I had gloves for her children while shivering on camera. That film aired on Austin TV and is still on YouTube today. It was like a rocket blast. My phone rang off the hook.

I was asked on TV, with the wind chill plumping, what I needed. I said coats, blankets, socks, sweaters, sleeping bags, and sweaters; as you can see, gloves are for these kids. And Bibles. One Austin attorney bought every sleeping bag Walmart had, around 25.

None of this was scripted. I began to pray, "Lord, I can't wait to see what you will do by noon today."

In time, I asked over 400 Central Texas churches of all denominations for Bibles. Less than ten gave away free copies of the Word of God. That night, I sat on a downtown curb by the Salvation Army and said, "Austin, we have a problem."

I soon got a call from Gene Bender, the manager of Austin's most prominent Christian radio station KIXL. We met for lunch at the Night Hawk at my suggestion. He laid out his plans. We've been looking for a local grassroots boots-on-the-ground ministry to support, and we'd like your organization to be that ministry.

While he lays out his plans, I think I have no ministry. I have no organization. I'm just a hayseed cowboy handing out a few Bibles that happened to have his picture in the paper. I will be yesterday's news in a week.

He then shares that KIXL would like to do two things. First, we will offer a 30-minute daily morning radio program between Charles Stanley and Adrian Roger. Now, I know he's confused me with someone else.

In closing, Mr. Bender said, I read the article on you giving your coat to a homeless man; if we promoted a coat drive for your "ministry," how many do you think we could raise by Christmas Eve? It was already the week after Thanksgiving. I said 700. I thought seven was an excellent Christian number.

I wept when I got to my pickup in the Night Hawk parking lot. "Lord, I just lied to that man. I don't know if we can raise one coat. And who am I to be on the radio between those two giants of the faith. I'm not a preacher."

I was aware I was just a messenger boy. I would pray, "Lord, let me get out of Your way; I'll mess this whole thing up."

The drive raised over 15,000 coats, blankets, sweaters, socks, sleeping bags, and more by Christmas Eve. Four years later, that number grew to 128,000 items.

I had no volunteers. It was just me and a bunch of folks in need. And my three sons, Aaron, Josh, and Adam, on weekends.

After I started my live radio broadcast five days a week, over 500 people volunteered. The other local television stations would quickly ask to film me feeding and clothing the needy, especially when a cold front was coming. The more severe a storm was, the more they showed up.

Randy Willis and Doc Washburn KIXL

All of this occurred within three months. The Lord has ways of doing the math I never dreamed of.

I figured this thing had grown about as much as it could. I was wrong.

I never had difficulty getting clothes or food. HEB never turned me down for smoked turkeys and other items for an annual Thanksgiving Dinner for the homeless. A local dry cleaner cleans everything free.

I figured the worst thing a company could do was say no. They couldn't shoot me, although I'm sure a couple would have liked to.

I read about a man who had done well selling drugs, no, not kind. His name was Jack Eckerd. He was the head of the Eckerd Drug Store chain, the oldest of the major drugstore companies in the U.S. He was a pilot in the Army Air Corp

237

in World II like my father, Darrell Royal, and Bro. JB Young. And I read he was a Christian.

Let's see if he's a member in good standing of the so-called "Greatest Generation," I might have a chance. I sat down and wrote a list of seven items that could be found in any of his drug stores and asked if he would consider donating a dozen of each. I knew I would never hear back from him, and I was right. He never answered my letter, called, or had a representative call. No giant company has time to respond to an unknown person like me.

A month passed when I received a shipment filled with 1,000 toothbrushes, toothpaste, soap, deodorant, and every item on my "wish list," 7,000 total items. When I get to Heaven, I will ask the Lord if I have any tiny reward; please give it to Jack Eckert and one other man. We were out of used Bibles and new ones our budget would allow us to purchase.

My radio show had become widespread in Central Texas, and Christmas was near. I asked my Pastor, Dr. Ralph Smith, if he would appear and bring a Christmas message. During that program, I sent out a plea for Bibles. Once again, I had no problems getting used clothes and food, but Bibles were a different issue.

Then I received the attached letter from Dr. Smith mentioning, as if it were a footnote, he wrote, "We're in the process of preparing some new Bibles, and as soon as they are completed, we would be more than happy to give you some copies."

When you're the largest church in Central Texas with over 14,000 members, you can own a printing press and print the no longer copywritten King James Version of the Bible.

238

Lord, give that other tiny share to Dr. Smith. That "some copies" grew into thousands. That ended my use of the NIV (Nearly Inspired Version).

Ralph M. Smith, Th.D.
Pastor

Hyde Park Baptist Church
3901 Speedway / Austin, Texas 78751 - 4699

December 2, 1993

Mr. Randy Willis
P.O. Box 15123
Austin, TX 78761

Dear Randy, my friend:

Thank you for letting me be on your radio broadcast. You were so kind to invite me. I counted it a real privilege to bring a message on the Christmas theme.

My prayer is with your work. We're in the process of preparing some new Bibles, and as soon as they are completed, we would be more than happy to give you some copies. I just don't have them ready and that's why we haven't given them to you sooner. We do want to continue to help and participate in your ministry.

Remember me when you pray. I count it a special privilege to be your pastor and friend.

Your friend,

Ralph M. Smith

RMS:jld

I asked Bob Edd Shotwell, the Minister of Education and head of the Hyde Park School System, if he would consider having the elementary students prepare Christmas stockings for the kids at the Salvation Army. He said yes. The kids and teachers prepared 400 brown paper bags with one each of the items I had received from Jack Eckerd and a KJV Bible in each bag.

They also added fruit and candy. A few students met me at the Salvation Army with their parents. Each child had a hand-wrapped gift, too, and they handed them to a child face to face in line, wishing them a Merry Christmas.

When I left the Salvation that day, all I could say was, "Who is like the Lord our God, Holy, Holy, Holy art thou," over and over and over.

The Lord had multiplied my meager "loaves and fishes." It would not be the last time.

Hyde Park students are ready to give Christmas gifts.
The Salvation Army Austin, Texas.

Hyde Park students giving Christmas gifts.
The Salvation Army Austin, Texas

☆ ☆ ☆

Hyde Park students giving Christmas gifts.
The Salvation Army Austin, Texas

☆ ☆ ☆

Two children that Hyde Park kids gave Christmas gifts.
The Salvation Army Austin, Texas.

243

On Christmas Eve, my three sons were with their mother. I loaded all the brown paper bag Christmas stockings I had left over into my pickup and some new ones.

When I arrived on a cold evening, several homeless men and women asked me why I was doing this on Christmas Eve.

"Let me tell you why," I smiled.

✫   ✫   ✫

In 1992, Dr. Marvin Olasky, a University of Texas Journalism professor, contacted me. He was working on a book entitled *Compassionate Conservatism*.

He had read about Operation Warm Heart in the Austin American Statesman. We began to feed and clothe those in need in Austin six days a week. We also gave out thousands of Bibles.

Dr. Olasky asked if he could go with me to the streets of Austin. While we fed the homeless and gave out Bibles, he asked me many questions and later quoted me in his book. George W. Bush wrote the forward.

The book eventually helped define "compassionate conservatism" concerning welfare and social policy. In 1995, Olasky became an occasional advisor to Texas gubernatorial candidate George W. Bush. Bush made faith-based programs a significant component of his 2000 presidential campaign, and Olasky's academic work helped form the basis for Bush's "compassionate conservatism."

Olasky also asked me if I would guest lecture in his journalism classes at The University of Texas, which I did. During those talks, he asked if any students would like to go to the streets of Austin and into the jails with me. Those who said yes were required to write a paper about that adventure for the class. They also got credit for their paper.

Randy Willis is on the far left.
Travis County Correctional Complex in Del Valle.
I had been invited the year before to speak twice a month at the Travis County Correctional Complex in Del Valle and

245

the Austin downtown jail by Senior Chaplain Tommy McIntosh. On this day (me on the left), I invited prisoners to come forward and give their testimonies. All Bibles had to go through the Chaplain. I was not allowed to directly hand them out. That was not the Chaplain's rule but the county.

I requested Senior Chaplain Tommy McIntosh approve me to speak to two additional groups, those convicted of the most serious crimes and the women's unit. I would eventually get the opportunity to talk to both.

Only five convicted male felons came when I got the approval. These men would soon be transferred to the State Penitentiary in Huntsville. I suspected they came only to get out of their confinement. The setting was like nothing I had experienced before. Two armed guards stood on the other side of the bars, watching every move I made in a tiny room. Only I was allowed in the room with them.

After I spoke, one of the inmates put his hand on my shoulder. I heard the guards move. I thought they were going to shoot him. The inmate wept and accepted Christ as his Lord and Savior. I glanced at the guards to ensure they were comfortable with the scene. One of the guards was crying, too. Then, another inmate began to weep. He, too, accepted Christ.

Soon, I was allowed to speak in the women's unit. Unlike the more dangerous scene above, I was allowed to bring a few volunteers, but they all had to be women.

At the end of the service, Evelyn Davison, who had her own ministry, said, I've never seen anything like this. Nor had I. The entire room began to praise Jesus. Evelyn later asked me, "What do you call this, a revival?

"The Holy Spirit," I said. It would not be the last time He showed up. When the less of me showed up, the more of Him showed up.

As I've grown older, I consider myself a follower of Christ and never use a denominational tag. And I rarely use the word God, but Jesus or Christ instead, for too many believe a tree is a god, they are god, and a movie star is a god. I know that Jesus, the Christ, is God incarnate, God in the flesh. No one should confuse Him with their many man-made gods. And don't get me started on those using the word "Christian" today or a cross around their necks.

Over two hundred women made decisions for Christ that day at Travis County Correctional Complex.

In my excitement that night, I called my mother. She was my number one encourager. Mama had the gift of encouragement. As I shared the women's responses, my mother became very quiet. That was usual for her. I ask her, "Is everything okay?"

After a long pause, she poured out her heart. "I've tried so many times to witness about Jesus. Every time I do, I forget the Scriptures and get confused, and I cannot explain the plan of salvation. I get nervous. I've never led anyone to Jesus."

I realized in my braggadocios excitement I was saying look at what I have done (and you haven't). Mama's words broke my heart.

I shared 1 Corinthians 12:12 with her. There is one body of Christ, but many parts. "Mama, I may have been the load mouth for a brief moment today, but you are the heart. Without the heart pumping the blood, all other parts die.

247

"And mother, without you, there would be no me." That truth was physical and spiritual, for she poured Jesus into me more by example than words. You could see Jesus in my mother's eyes with her kindness and empathy. I would gladly exchange less of the mouth for more of the heart any day.

That ended my use of estimates, numbers, and statistics regarding how many accepted "Christ as Savior." The Lord's count is the only one that matters.

☆　　☆　　☆

On the street, I was confronted by what seemed to be every belief on planet Earth, and they all wanted to debate. I followed Christ's example in the wilderness when Satan tried to draw him into a debate.

Christ only answered with Scripture, beginning each time with, "It is written." Christ did no name-calling. Now, I figure if Christ did not debate Satan, I wouldn't debate his family members.

That was not hard. What was more challenging, at least for me, was not to bring up the possibility of where that might be headed.

Two Jehovah's Witnesses asked if they could speak to me one night. I said sure. I already knew who they represented because of their dress and was familiar with their pitch. I listened politely, and when they finished, I said, "Thank you for sharing your beliefs."

Now, let me tell you about Jesus. I quoted verbatim only Scriptures. Within 30 minutes, the three of us held hands as they accepted the Lord Jesus Christ as their Lord and Savior.

The sword of the Holy Spirit, the Word of God, is all needed to pierce the most challenging heart. None of our cleverness of words will draw them. Only the Holy Spirit can do that, and He does it with His two-edged sword that pierces both directions, the mighty Sword of the Spirit, the infallible, inerrant Word of God.

Randy Willis The Salvation Army

Jimmy Pritchard, Evelyn, and Van Davison

I only had a couple of rules. We never accepted cash or checks. We had no checking account for the so-called "ministry." No volunteer nor I was ever compensated financially. I have lived by that rule until this day.

There was no litmus test to help us feed and clothe the needy. Some were atheists. I allowed every denomination on the planet. Well, maybe not one, those guys who handle those snakes. Some of the atheists got saved. But there were two things I did restrict, those who preached Jesus and those who baptized.

I took advantage of several Southern Baptist ordained ministers who volunteered. I had no time to study the theology of the others, so I went with what I knew. I never told anyone this, for that would have become the focal point in the newspapers.

One of the volunteers was Pastor Jimmy Pritchard. He died on February 24, 2021, of COVID-19. As I read his long list of incredible accomplishments, one jumped out at me: "Baptized over 2,600 new believers."

I thought that was inaccurate because when I started Operation Warm Heart in 1991, Jimmy was the first Pastor to volunteer. It was a ministry to the last, the least, and the lost, and many of them Jimmy baptized. The folks of Samaria, aka the outcast, hurting, rejected, and needy of Austin, were our "target market" spoken of in Acts 1:8.

Jimmy and I would speak, although he was the only one ordained, so he did all the baptizing. He baptized hundreds of people in the streets of Austin in a year or two. We were not allowed to baptize in the jails. He was also the Pastor of Congress Avenue Baptist Church in South Austin.

No one knows the number saved because our church clerk, Jesus, is the only one with accurate accounting. Only one book counts, the Lamb's Book of Life.

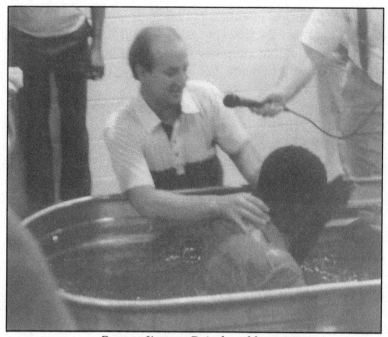

Pastor Jimmy Pritchard baptizing
at the Salvation Army in Austin.

Randy Willis (top left), Jimmy Pritchard, and Evelyn Davison with Bibles sharing Christ.

Evelyn Davison and Texas Governor Greg Abbott
Evelyn Davison was America's Honorary Prayer Coordinator for the National Day of Prayer for 40 years. Former Texas Governor Rick Perry called her his "Prayer Mother." After my mother's death, she became my surrogate mother and the #1 Prayer Warrior formally held by Mama.

253

Somehow, someway, the Lord always provides. I'd given Him dozens of suggestions concerning Operation Warm Heart and my needs. To this day, He has never used one of my suggestions.

We accepted food, clothes, and Bibles. If you go through your closet and take out the items you have not worn in a year, you will discover that you will probably never wear them.

Local Austin fast-food restaurants donated what they had not sold by the end of the day. Mostly, fried chicken, pizzas, and bakery items. Volunteers picked the food up.

Find a need, find a hurt, and meet those needs and hurts in the name of Jesus and watch what He does.

"He who loses his life for My sake will find it."

Jesus said, "I was hungry and you gave Me food; I was thirsty and you gave Me drink; I was a stranger and you took Me in; I *was* naked and you clothed Me; I was sick and you visited Me; I was in prison and you came to Me…

"Assuredly, I say to you, in as much as you did *it* to one of the least of these My brethren, you did *it* to Me." (Matthew 25)

Randy Willis is top center.

Aaron Willis is on the top left, Josh Willis is on the
center, and Adam Willis is on the right.

255

JOSH AND AARON WILLIS

Josh Willis and Aaron Willis

ADAM, RANDY, JOSH, AND AARON WILLIS

Adam, Randy, Josh, and Aaron Willis
The Salvation Army Austin, Texas

256

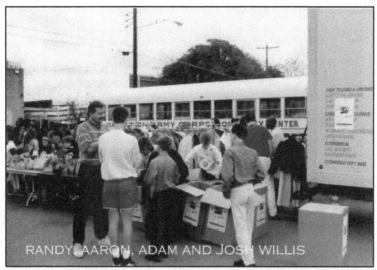

Randy, Aaron, Adam, and Josh Willis
The Salvation Army in Austin, Texas

The books on the table are Bibles.
Randy Willis setting up for a big day.

Operation Warm Heart Volunteers

Operation Warm Heart Volunteers

Randy Willis handing out the fried chicken.
They called me "Chicken Man."

Randy Willis 8th Street near Red River in Austin.

259

Randy Willis The Salvation Army. Austin, Texas
Adam Willis is on the far left.

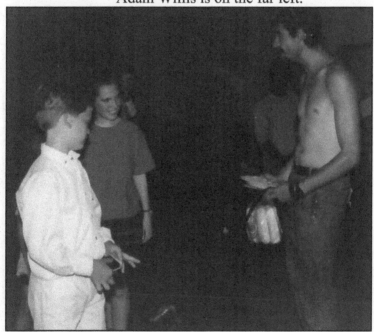

Adam Willis left handing out Bibles.

My friend Diana Lynn and her daughter Leah helping me feed the needy in Austin. They helped many times. I forget the name of this dear young Pastor.

Leah Ashley feeding the needy in Austin. I'm not saying that if you helped me feed the needy in Austin, you'd become a TV star, but then again, Leah did.

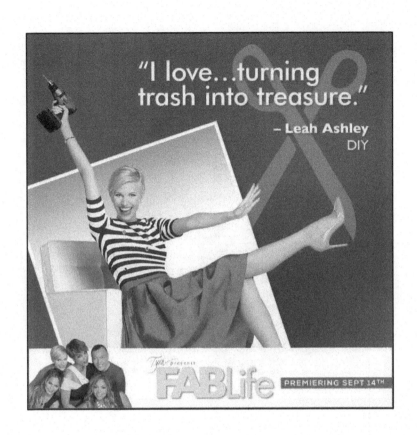

✫   ✫   ✫

263

Randy Willis
Children's Miracle Network Telethon

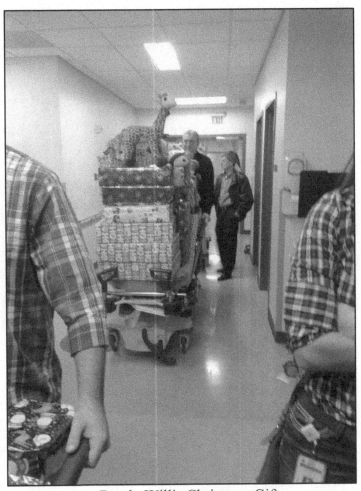

Randy Willis Christmas Gifts
Dell Children's Medical Center
Austin, Texas

Randy Willis Christmas Gifts
Dell Children's Medical Center
Randy Willis, top left

Randy Willis
Texas Baptist Children's Home
Round Rock, Texas

Randy Willis
Texas Baptist Children's Home
Round Rock, Texas

Aaron, Adam, and Josh Willis
Children's Miricle Network Telethon

Randy Willis Austin Home

☆　　　☆　　　☆

269

TELETHON FOOTNOTES

CHILDREN'S HOSPITAL OF AUSTIN
AT BRACKENRIDGE

Volume 4, No. 3   Summer 1990

1990 TELETHON MARKS RECORD SUCCESS

A record $760,000 was raised by the 1990 Children's Miracle Network Telethon in Austin for Children's Hospital. "The Telethon was successful because of the support and hard work of hundreds of volunteers and ongoing support from the staff. Everyone worked with purpose and dedication throughout the entire year and at the Telethon," stated Pam Willeford, Chairman of the 1990 Children's Miracle Network Telethon.

The KVUE 24 crew, Judy Maggio and Robert Hadlock, deserve special thanks for their energy and enthusiasm for hosting the 21-hour Telethon live from the

Telethon Hosts Judy Maggio and Robert Hadlock and Telethon Chairman Pam Willeford were all smiles. This was a sure sign of the rewards of a job well done and the end of a successful Telethon.

Emily Lambert, one of the Miracle Children visits with Skippy during the Telethon.

Marriott at the Capitol Ballroom. Bob Cole of KASE 101 FM and Deborah Duncan of KVUE Channel 24 delighted audiences with live coverage of the Telethon from Highland Mall.

The phone pledges this year were up in part due to incentives offered to those calling in. For pledges of $500 or more, one free airline ticket was given by Continental Airlines to anywhere they fly in the U.S. The Music for Miracles tape was given to those persons calling in a $50 or more pledge. A big thanks goes out to the satellite phone banks for raising over $5800 for Children's Hospital in Austin. These satellites include Gastrop, Blanco, Burnet, Dripping Springs, Elgin, Freder-

icksburg, Georgetown, Giddings, Lakeway, Lockhart, Marble Falls and San Marcos.

"The continued success of the Children's Miracle Network Telethon in Austin demonstrates the priority that the people of Central Texas place on providing the best healthcare available to their children," states Bitsy Henderson, Director of Development for Brackenridge Hospital. "Our thanks to Pam Willeford and her dedicated group of volunteers, to Sandi Mizirl, Telethon Coordinator, and Peggy Cooley, Assistant Telethon Coordinator, for an outstanding year."

The Children's Miracle Network Telethon originated again this year in Disney-

Continued on page 8

Adam Willis and Josh Willis
in front with white shirts on.

Adam Willis is above and below.
Over 30 years feeding and clothing the needy.

271

Adam Willis
The Salvation Army

Bum Phillips, Earl Cambell, Randy Willis, and Tony
Dorsett. Benefit at The Headliners Club.
Austin, Texas

APPENDIX A
THE LOGOS OR ME, MYSELF, AND I

Have I questioned the plenary inspiration of the Word of God (Logos)? Do I believe the Book from Genesis 1:1 to the maps in the back—well, maybe not the maps. Have I ever doubted the inerrancy and infallibility of the Book, the Bible?

The answer is no, so shall I write about how wonderful I have been? The Apostle Paul writes in 1 Timothy 1:15-1, "This is a faithful saying and worthy of all acceptance, that Christ Jesus came into the world to save sinners, of whom I am chief."

The Apostle Paul said he was numero uno, as we say in the Texas Hill Country—number one, as we try to be at my three favorite colleges, Texas State University, The University of Texas, and LSU—a Chief as a pop star identifies herself—I know, you got it. Good, I was running out of bad metaphors.

The apostle Paul considers himself the "foremost" of sinners. Wow, then where do I stand? Many would say that's not positive thinking. The truth is, we all fall short of the Glory of God.

So here I am, believing every Word in God's Owner's Manual for my life, but I want to control said life.

I bought a GMC pickup with an owner's manual a few years ago. I've searched from cover to cover and cannot find where I can drive drunk at a hundred miles an hour with my grandkids in the front seat. But, officer, I have the right to

273

drive as I deem best since I own that truck. Tell the judge that.

The first lie ever spoken on this earth was by the fallen angel Lucifer in the Garden of Eden, "Did God say."

I've heard "Did God Say" packaged and repackaged in hundreds of ways in the press and pulpit. Lucifer, known as Satan today, wants us to think we can't trust God. So Satan attacks the accuracy of the Word of God. Satan wants us to think we can't believe the Word of God, the Bible.

Then Satan tells Eve another lie, "You will not surely die." Satan wants us to believe there is no punishment for rebelling against God—sin. Satan wants us to think there is no eternal separation from God because of sin—hell. Tell the Judge of the universe that.

Satan explains to Eve why God lied. "For God knows that in the day you eat of it, your eyes will be opened, and you will be like God, knowing good and evil."

Now, Eve, you will be enlightened. Reminds me of what we were told in college if we did LSD.

Satan declares to Eve what he said of himself, "You will be like the Most High."

It's the same lie we hear every day. You can be like God; you can be in control. You are your own God. You are a God. It's all about me, myself, and I. No one can tell me what I can and can not do. You are in control of your body. Not God.

I've tried being in control. Spoiler alert—it does not work. You'll lose your peace, joy, purpose, and life. And God's plan for you and your resurrected body after the rapture. That will be an improvement in my case.

Hollywood's Ozempic prescriptions will be no more.

I remind myself daily that any decision I surrender to the Lord will have the best results. Easier said than done, I know. But Lord, I want to do it *My Way* like Frank Sinatra sang. It's almost as if He says, let me know how that works for you. No, He didn't say that to me.

☆   ☆   ☆

I've been blessed to have read and heard some of the best preachers of Jesus since the Apostle Paul. Billy Graham, the greatest evangelist since Paul, was the first famous one to influence me. As a teenager, I never missed his Crusades on TV. They still never get old.

During my first year at Southwest Texas State College (university the following year) in San Marcos, I stopped at a print shop on Hopkins Street to have copies made.

While I waited, I thumbed through a chrome metal bookshelf you could twirl 360 degrees with 99-cent paperback books. I debated if I could afford one. When my Xerox copies were ready, I said, "What the heck" and bought three. They were *Peace with God, The Jesus Generation*, and *World Aflame*. I devoured them. They are still on my bookshelf near my desk.

My mother preferred Billy Graham's wife, Ruth Graham's books. Mother read them all and loved them. I later did, too, and her daughter, Anne Graham-Lotz's books, especially her book *The Magnificent Obsession*.

I discovered Charles Haddon Spurgeon's *All of Grave* and his other books in my early twenties.

275

But another who was influenced by Spurgeon and was born on the same day as I was, December 19, precisely 40 years before W.A. Criswell became my favorite famous pastor. I never met him, but he has over 4,000 sermons online, so I feel like I know him. I've never read or listened to anyone with his intellect in the Word.

I've heard Dr. Criswell's sermon, *Whether We Live or Die,* which includes a brief summary of Spurgeon's "The Downgrade in the Churches," ten-plus times. The message is more valid today than ever.

Dr. Criswell's *The Scarlet Thread Through the Bible* runs throughout the Bible, which is another favorite. He traces the scarlet thread of redemption from the blood of covering after the fall in the Garden of Eden to Calvary's Cross and the blood-washed multitude standing before the throne of God in eternity. It has blessed me numerous times. It will bless your life.

Adrian Rogers would be a close second to W.A. Criswell. And J. Vernon McGee, Mark Bubeck, Charles Stanley, E.V. Hill, Scott Tatum, D.L. Lowrie, and others have blessed me. All of these men are in Heaven except D.L. Lowrie. He is another one of my favorites. You can follow him on Facebook. He is still preaching Jesus.

Dr. Charles Stanley's six-part series *After Brokenness Then What* changed my life. Dr. Jody Unruh with Hyde Park Counseling Center loaned me a copy after my fiancé died of anorexia. My Pastor, Dr. Ralph Smith, recommended Dr. Unruh to me. If you have ever experienced a significant loss of a loved one, this series will help you get through the pain as none other I've ever listened to. Dr. Stanley was a great Pastor, too.

Dr. Unruh helped me move on from the tragic loss of my fiancé through Christian counseling. Dr. Smtih told me she was "spiritually blessed," and she was. Dr. Unruh was the only counselor I ever saw. She had studied at Dr. Charles Stanley's church. I decided to date again, but only Christian women rooted in a Bible-believing church.

It was a good decision, except there was one thing that neither Dr. Unruh nor I knew. I had built a 20-foot high, thick stone fence around my heart. I would never allow myself to be destroyed again in a romantic relationship.

Consequently, I either sabotaged or fled unexpectedly when someone became too close. It's a character flaw I have never gotten past. I'm sure a million books have been written on this subject, but I never cared to read one. It answers one of my most often-asked questions: Why aren't you married?

My first date after the tragedy.

I was playing golf at a Darrell Royal charity golf tournament, *The Ben Willie Darrell*, at Barton Creek Country Club when Coach Royal asked me after Edith, his wife, called; Edith wants to know, "Why aren't you married?" I had asked an acquaintance of hers for a date.

Due diligence was in action. I almost said, "Tell Miss Edith, Coach, all the posters of me have been removed from the post office bulletin board."

I didn't wish to get into the details, so I gave the classic go-to answer, "I just never found the right person."

Willie Nelson turned as he teed up and said, "You know

why divorces are so expensive?" He smiled and added, "Because they're worth it."

Randy Willis and Willie Nelson. Golfing at
Barton Creek Country Club Austin, Texas

Willie Nelson, Randy Willis, Darrell Royal
Barton Creek Country Club Austin, Texas

The pastors of the local churches I have been honored and blessed to attend and belong to had just as much, if not more, influence on my life than the famous ones.

We attended Longleaf Baptist Church in Longleaf, Louisiana, until we moved to Texas when I was four.

I have belonged to four churches in the last seven decades: Temple Baptist in Clute, Texas, where I "hit the sawdust trail" on a Wednesday night, August 24, 1958. I was only eight, but I recall that night as if it were five minutes ago.

During my high school years, I belonged to Second Baptist in Angleton, Texas, and was primarily inactive due to my obligation to work on the farm.

After college, I joined First Baptist in Wimberley, Texas, where the pastor, Brother J.B. Young, was my surrogate father. He flew World War II's first combat mission early on December 7, 1941, from Hickam Field at Pearl Harbor. I loved that man.

Brother Young was one of the three best men I have ever known. The other two were University of Texas football Coach Darrell K Royal and my Dad. All three men were in the United States Army Air Corps in World War II. The Greatest Generation is not a cliché to me.

When I moved to a foreign country with my passport in hand, Austin, Texas, for the first and only time, I joined Hyde Park Baptist Church. The Pastor was Dr. Ralph Smith. Dr. Smith and Associate Pastor Paul Stephens were my friends, but Paul became one of my closest friends.

In 1990, I invited Ralph Smith and his wife, Bess, to dinner at Beijing Restaurant in Austin and Paul Stephens and his wife, Joy.

Paul took the photos. Joy was seated to the back right. It was Bess's Birthday. Other invited guests were with Campus Crusade for Christ and other ministries. Dr. Smith mailed me a gracious letter afterward.

281

I am seated at the far end of the table to the left. Beijing Restaurant Austin, Texas. Dr. Smith's wife, Bess Smith's Birthday.

Ralph M. Smith, Th. D.
Pastor

Hyde Park Baptist Church
3901 Speedway / Austin, Texas 78751 - 4699

November 20, 1990

Mr. Randy Willis
President

Dear Randy:

Bess and I want to thank you for inviting us to have dinner with
you all last night. The meal was delicious.

We've never been in the Beijing Restaurant, and it was very
special. You   are a precious blessing
to me and our church. I especially want to thank you for all you
do for missions and for your friendship to Paul Stephens. As you
know, I think that he's one of the greatest guys in the world.

Thank you again.

Sincerely,

Ralph M. Smith

RMS:jld

Hyde Park Baptist Church would deepen my faith and
support my efforts beyond the call of duty in feeding and
clothing the needy with Operation Warm Heart, which I
founded.

After I informed him of an error I had made, Dr. Smith
told me, "Allow yourself four mistakes a day, and the ones
you don't use today carry over to tomorrow." I'm up to
several thousand allowed mistakes.

December 28, 1992

Mr. Randy Willis
P.O. Box 15123
Austin, TX 78761

Dear Randy:

Thank you so very much for providing the 500 label sets for the New Testaments that we plan to distribute. What a generous and appreciated gift this is!

Randy, I really miss seeing you, and hope to see a lot more of you in this new year. Bless you for all that you do to help the homeless and hurting. I am very proud of you.

May the New Year bring you and your family abundant joy and happiness.

Your pastor and friend,

Ralph M. Smith

Thank you for being my friend.

In 1989, a friend, Leah Kay Lyle, decided to run for Miss Texas. She won.

Dr. W.A. Criswell asked her to speak at First Baptist Dallas when the Baptist Standard ran her photo on the cover.

284

Leah Kay Lyle and Randy Willis
Children's Miracle Network Telethon

BAPTIST STANDARD

August 2, 1989

Leah Kay Lyle, Miss Texas
... beautiful on the inside, too.

Page 5

My pastor, Ralph Smith, called me and said, "Criswell is having your friend speak at his church. And you're a member here. And she's your friend, right?" I wondered when he would get to the point. "So, will you ask her to speak here, too?" She did, and her testimony was incredible.

I invited a small church group to lunch with Leah Kay and me at Beijing Restaurant after church, including Paul and Joy Stephens, Hyde Park's Minister of Music Joe Carrell, and

286

his wife, Barbara. Hyde Park's choir was the best I'd ever heard. Dr. Smith had previous plans. I received a kind card from Joe and Barbara Carrrell.

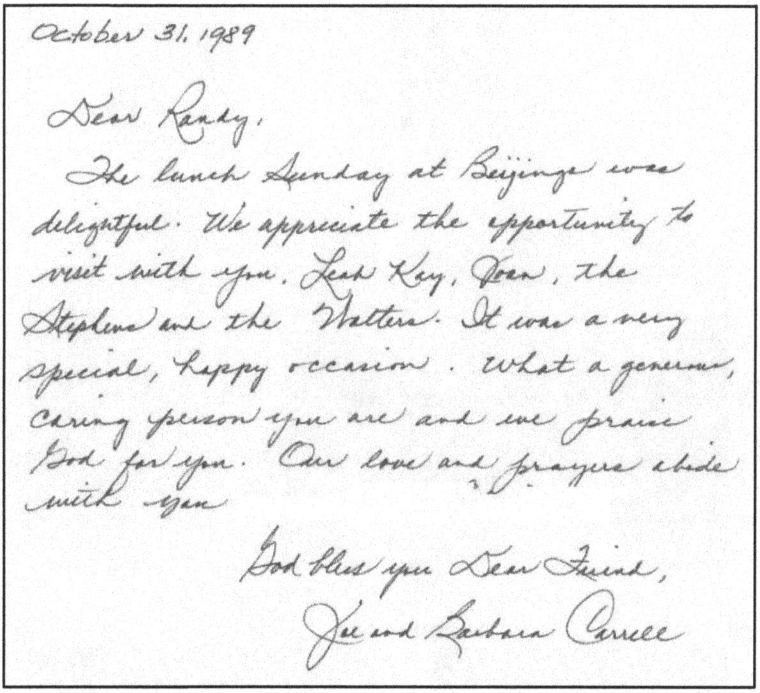

October 31, 1989

Dear Randy,

The lunch Sunday at Beijing was delightful. We appreciate the opportunity to visit with you, Leah Kay, Joan, the Stephens and the Watters. It was a very special, happy occasion. What a generous, caring person you are and we praise God for you. Our love and prayers abide with you

God bless you Dear Friend,
Joe and Barbara Carrell

★ ★ ★

Randy Willis and Leah Kay Lyle
Austin, Texas Skyline

YOU'RE INVITED TO PERFORM A LITTLE MIRACLE.

Robert Hadlock and Judy Maggio with KVUE-TV together with Skippy (of Children's Hospital of Austin) welcome Randy Willis, owner of Contract Blind and Drapery, and Leah Kay Lyle, director of Public Relations for Contract Blind and Drapery.

Contract Blind & Drapery, Inc. invites you to help make miracles happen for Children's Hospital of Austin at Brackenridge. Fill in the attached donation form and send with your contribution to Children's Hospital. Contract Blind and Drapery will *match dollar for dollar* every contribution. *You* can be a miracle maker, too!

Children's Miracle Network Telethon

Randy Willis and Leah Kay Lyle
Children's Miracle Network Telethon

Dr. Smith often referred to First Baptist Dallas and Prestonwood Baptist in Plano as Hyde Park's little mission churches.

He once told me that in 35 years of counseling people, one word came up in every counseling session. The word was "if." If I had done this. If I had not done that.

Brother Paul Stephens and I would meet for lunch at The Night Hawk Restaurant once a week. It had incredible food,

289

fair prices, and a staff that had worked there for over 40 years in some cases.

I once invited a notorious Austin Street Preacher to join us. When our lunch was delivered to our table, the street preacher said, "Ya'll pay, and I'll pray." So, I did the "Christian" thing; I never invited him again.

Ralph Smith and Paul Stephens baptized my three sons. All three were born at St. David's Medical Center on IH 35 and 32nd Street in Austin. From there, you can see the tall steeple of Hyde Park Baptist Church in the distance, where all three of my sons were baptized. The irony was not lost on me.

My Son Aaron Willis was baptized by Paul Stephens. Hyde Park Baptist Church Austin, Texas

Over the years, when I drive by St. David's on the highway, I look west toward that steeple and thank the Lord for the miracle of birth and the new birth. My youngest three

290

granddaughters were born there, too. Violet Jean Willis was born there this year. I pray they, too, look at "that" steeple and know the meaning of the new birth.

SOUTHWESTERN BAPTIST THEOLOGICAL SEMINARY
P.O. Box 22000/Fort Worth, Texas 76122
(817) 923-1921

Scott L. Tatum
Professor of Preaching

April 26, 1982

Mr. and Mrs. Randy Willis
P. O. Box 351
Wimberly, Texas 78676

Dear Randy and Becky:

Thank you for your hospitality and for the privilege of having such a lovely meal in your home during our recent revival together. It was a real joy to get to know you more personally. I hope that our paths will cross often in the years that lie ahead.

Randy, thank you for sharing such interesting materials about your family history and especially about the Strothers. These are special people whom God has used in a marvelous way. I am glad to be related to them through my Aunt Effie. I know you are equally happy to claim all of them.

Cordially yours,

Scott L. Tatum

SLT/cam

Dr. Scott Tatum, a friend who married into our family many years ago, was pastor at Hyde Park before Dr. Ralph Smith and recommended the church to me. Scott married the

291

daughter of Willie Strother, Effie, a descendant of Rev. Joseph Willis, like me.

We became friends in 1982 when he stayed at my home in Wimberley when he preached a revival at First Baptist Wimberley.

I asked Dr. Tatum once how you know if you're called to preach.

"If you can keep from it, don't," he said.

A friend who shall remain unnamed (Glen Hardwick) claims I have never attended anything but Southern Baptist Churches. I know, I've done the math; that's five Southern Baptist Churches, counting Longleaf.

But Glen's wrong; I've attended funerals and weddings at other denominations. My friend Glen is a Methodist but not devout, so don't hold that against the Methodist. I doubt he has ever heard of John Wesley.

I "backslid" a few times by attending two churches, not Southern Baptist: Shoreline Church, with Rob Koke at the helm, because it was near my home and was known for its music in North Austin, and Celebration Church north of Austin.

Both are non-denominational churches. Both churches have incredible pastors, staff, and members. And I loved the music, although some songs seemed to be 30 minutes long.

Rob Koke's services also ran past noon. No wonder with that music. That's a sin, especially if the Dallas Cowboys are playing. Rob often admonished us not to leave before the alter call to beat the Baptist to Luby's because they were already there. That reminded me to sit in the back row, knowing I would need a restroom break at noon.

Of the two, I attended Celebration Church the least because of the distance. You can tell I hate driving long distances. When I first visited Celebration, I discovered the church aligned with my "theology" when I noticed they served Community Coffee from Louisiana. Shoreline had a Yankee brand, Starbucks. I have prayed for Shoreline ever since.

Pastor Champion greeted everyone in the lobby and drank coffee with them before church, although I was sure that was a sin. I can't recall the chapter and verse. I always understood that could only be done at the end of the service. Perhaps that's a sin, too, today, since many mega-churches don't do that.

I soon discovered Celebration's pastor, Joe Champion, was anointed when he mentioned he'd played football at LSU.

APPENDIX B
CHOOSE YOUR DESTINY

In 1829, George Wilson was found guilty of six charges and was given the death sentence. However, Wilson had influential friends who petitioned President Andrew Jackson for a pardon. Jackson granted the pardon, which was brought to the prison and given to Wilson.

To everyone's surprise, Wilson said, "I am going to hang."

There had never been a refusal to a pardon, so the courts didn't know what to do. The case went to the Supreme Court, and Chief Justice John Marshall ruled, saying, "A pardon is a piece of paper, the value of which depends upon the acceptance by the person implicated. If he does not accept the pardon, then he must be executed."

God loves you, and, yes, He has provided a pardon for you and me, paid for with Christ's lifeblood, but you have the right to refuse the pardon for your sins.

Jesus was crucified between two thieves. One thief said yes to Jesus, but the other said no. One accepted the pardon, and the other refused.

The question to you and me today is the same as it was 2,000 years ago. Which thief on the cross are you? The one who said yes to God's pardon or the one who said no? I have chosen to say yes.

You have the same choice.

Come

The last invitation in the Word of God is in Revelation 22:17: "And the Spirit and the bride say, 'Come!' And let him who hears say, 'Come!' And let him who thirsts come. Whoever desires, let him take the water of life freely."

Are you thirsty? Then come. Let him who hears come. And, whosoever will, come.

That invitation is to you—to me—to "whosoever will"—everyone!

Bring your disappointments, bring your failures, bring your fears, bring your heartaches. The Holy Spirit says come to Jesus.

He loves you. He wants to save you. He *will* save you. Come to Jesus, and drink the water of life freely.

He suffered, He bled, He died because He loves you. Listen to the still, small voice of the Holy Spirit, bidding you come to Jesus.

Don't wait—come!

Look

"Look to Me, and be saved, All you ends of the earth!
For I am God, and there is no other."
(Isaiah 45:22)

"All you ends of the earth" includes the Aboriginal people of the Central Australian desert.
"All you ends of the earth" are those in darkest Africa.

"All you ends of the earth" are the isolated tribes in the Amazon rainforest in Brazil.

"All you ends of the earth" are presidents, world leaders, and kings.

"All you ends of the earth" is the polished lawyer, the gifted doctor, and the brilliant college professor.

"All you ends of the earth" is the prostitute, and the drug dealer, and the rapist, and the thief, and the murderer.

"All you ends of the earth" is you—and me.

God's Bible states, "So Moses made a bronze serpent, and put it on a pole; and so it was, if a serpent had bitten anyone when he looked at the bronze serpent, he lived."

Those who looked lived.
Those who looked were healed.
Those who looked were made whole.
Those who looked were saved.
They didn't wait until they were better people.
They didn't touch it.
They just looked.

Jesus tells us this is a picture of Him being lifted up on the cross. "And as Moses lifted up the serpent in the wilderness, even so must the Son of Man be lifted up, that whoever believes in Him should not perish but have eternal life." (John 3:14-15)

That bronze serpent represented the sin of the people. Christ was made sin for us.

Will you look to Jesus?—will you put your trust in Him?—the One who died for your sins.

Will you put your faith in Jesus?—the One who shed His life-blood for you—and me.

☆ ☆ ☆

My First Born Son Aaron Willis

Some years ago, my eldest son, Aaron, was in an automobile accident. His back was broken so severely that the doctors said he might not ever walk again.

After fusing several vertebrae in his lower back, he was able to begin the long task of healing from the spinal fusion surgery. He was encased in a rigid plastic back brace from his neck to his waist.

Later, his doctor finally agreed to let him briefly remove the brace and shower as long as someone was with him.

As I was driving to pick him and his brothers up for the weekend, unbeknownst to me, his brother, Josh, helped him remove the brace so he could take a hot shower in his shorts. Josh was with him but was much smaller than him at that time.

I stopped at the Austin post office on St. Johns, off IH 35, when a small voice said, "You need to go now."

I passed the post office and drove as fast as possible to Wimberley, an hour away, wondering what that warning was.

There were no cell phones then. As I entered the house,

I asked his mother where he was. She said in the shower.

I ran to it, and as soon as I entered the bathroom, he said, "Dad, I'm dizzy."

I stepped into the shower and placed my arms under his arms from his back. He immediately passed out.

.I told his younger brother to help me move him to a bed while their mother called 911. His dead weight was more than I could have ever imagined.

We got him onto the bed without reinjuring his back. I knew if he had fallen, he probably would have been paralyzed.

As I prayed, following the ambulance to the hospital's emergency room, I noticed the symbol on the ambulance's back.

It was the American Medical Association's (AMA) logo of a serpent wrapped around a staff.

The sign of healing medicine reminded me of the bronze serpent on the staff lifted up by Moses. Many Christians believe that's where the symbol originated.

But, more importantly, it reminded me of Jesus being lifted up on a cross for my son. God's son suffered in place of my son. I can't fathom love that great.

To this day, I cannot see that symbol without giving thanks to the Lord for that warning and the shed blood of Christ lifted high upon a cross for my sins, your sins, and the sins of the entire world.

Indeed, there can be no greater love than God giving His Son's life-blood for us.

When we arrived at the hospital, the doctors gave him intravenous (IV) fluids and two bottles of Gatorade for dehydration.

The hot shower, along with pain medication and dehydration, had caused his blood to rush to his feet and, thereby, faint.

Will you look to the One lifted up on a cross for you? Will you look to the Great Physician—Jesus—to heal you of all your pain?

Will you look to Jesus, who took your place on the cross and died for your sins?

Choose

As I said before, Jesus hung between two thieves on a cross. One rejected Him, but the other put his faith in Him.

"Will You remember me when You enter Your kingdom?" one thief asks. Jesus replied, "Assuredly, I say to you, today you will be with Me in Paradise." (Luke 23:43)

Both of those men were guilty. One put his trust in Jesus, and the other chose not to.
Again, the question is, which thief on the cross are you?

Now, there was the third cross that day. It was for another criminal named Barabbas, and he represents us.

Jesus was crucified on a cross meant for Barabbas—it was your cross, too—it was also my cross.

299

Jesus bore your cross and my cross. He took our place on that cross. The just for the unjust. The Righteous for the unrighteous. The sinless Lamb of God for the sinner.

Self-improvement will not qualify you for salvation, for God's Word says, "There is none righteous, no, not one." (Romans 3:10)

Comparing yourself to others will not work either, "for all have sinned and fall short of the glory of God." (Romans 3:23)

Doing your best cannot save you, for the Scriptures record, "But we are all like an unclean thing, And all our righteousnesses are like filthy rags." (Isaiah 64:6)

If you could be good enough to pay for your sins, ask yourself, why did Jesus have to die for you?

Come—come just as you are.

Will you say yes to Jesus—today?

There's a Scripture that I love, and it explains things very thoroughly.

"If thou shalt confess with thy mouth the Lord Jesus, and shalt believe in thine heart that God hath raised him from the dead, thou shalt be saved. For with the heart, man believeth unto righteousness; and with the mouth, confession is made unto salvation." (Romans 10:9-10)

You can settle this question in heaven and on earth by saying yes to Jesus—accepting His pardon, just as that one thief did on the cross. There are no prescriptive or mandated words. Praying is just talking to the Lord.

APPENDIX C
CHANGE YOUR DESTINY

If these words are how you feel in your heart, then pray:

"Heavenly Father,

I pray to You, asking for the forgiveness of my sins.

I confess with my mouth and believe with my heart that Jesus is Your Son, that He died on the cross at Calvary, and that I might be forgiven.

Father, I believe that Jesus rose from the dead, and I ask You to come into my life and be my personal Lord and Savior.

I repent of my sins and will surrender to You all the days of my life.

Because Your word is truth, I confess with my mouth that I am born again and cleansed by the blood of Jesus!

In Jesus' name, I pray. Amen!"

The most famous 25 words ever spoken: "For God so loved the world that He gave His only begotten Son, that whoever believes in Him should not perish but have everlasting life." (John 3:16)

"Whoever" is you—it's me—it's everyone.
Come to Jesus.
Look to Jesus.
Choose Jesus.
Today!

I would today be more still and listen for that still soft voice. Oh, that I would speak less and listen more.

Listen, He is speaking.
Look, He has manifested Himself.
Choose—say yes to Jesus—today.
You will never regret that decision.

—Randy Willis

☆   ☆   ☆

"He is no fool who gives what he cannot keep to gain what he cannot lose." —Jim Elliot

APPENDIX D
FIRE AND BRIMSTONE IN LOUISIANA

Strange how one event will harden one man's heart and melt another.

On Sunday, May 13, 1928, John Ford's silent film Hangman's House was released. And my first professional rodeo hero, Jim Shoulders, was born. But that was the only good news that day.

One of the most tragic events in Louisiana's history occurred within walking distance of our family home, The Ole Willis Home Place.

The events that would soon follow would shock the nation, according to *The New York Times*.

It was the middle of prohibition, which banned the manufacture, storage, transportation, sale, possession, and consumption of alcoholic beverages.

Governor Huey P. Long was asked by the mayor of Atlanta what he planned to do about the enforcement of the 18th Amendment, and he responded, "Not a damn thing."

But Rapides Parish, where my family had lived since 1828, was no New Orleans, dumbed the "liquor capital of America." It could be dangerous if you were a bootlegger or owned a Still. One thing more dangerous than operating one was operating one and not being white.

The Great Depression was a few months away, so there was plenty of money for an illegal visit to the corner liquor store known as a Moonshine Still. Rapides Parish's tall, thick, longleaf pines were rumored to have had several.

One of the Stills was within earshot of the Ole Willis Home Place, high up on a hill on Barber Creek. The Still was in the valley below, and the sounds of commerce would filter upwards through the fragrant piney woods.

My namesake and Grandpa Randall Lee "Rand" Willis had no issue with moonshine being down below at the end of a well-beaten path he often trod, but Grandma did. She believed Grandpa had cut that "broad is the way that leads to destruction" red dirt trail in more ways than one.

☆   ☆   ☆

Grandpa Rand and Uncle Howard Willis ca. 1930

I have no clue why Grandma thought that, although Grandpa drank a quart of hooch: white lightning, homebrew, firewater, or moonshine. Take your pick; they're all the same in the eyes of the local law enforcement and Grandma.

The fine folks at nearby Longleaf Baptist Church, where my family attended, included me until age four when we moved to Texas.

And nearby Amiable Baptist Church, my 4th Great-Grandfather Joseph Willis founded precisely one hundred years before, 1828, had an issue with the moonshine. Both of the churches would kick you to the red dirt curb if you even dream of having a drink of the Devil's Elixir.

The owner of the still was William Blackman. Grandpa was one of his best customers. Mr. Blackman's patch of woods was known as "Blackman Settlement." Mr. Blackman was called a [racial slur]." But Grandpa did not have a racist bone in his body, at least when it came to purchasing liquor. Grandpa called him Mr. Blackman.

When I was growing up, my Uncle Howard Willis was our family's master storyteller. We lived near Longleaf, Louisiana, and he lived up the road in Forest Hill, Louisiana.

Uncle Howard was the first to tell me of the tragic day, Sunday, May 13, 1928. He would not be the last.

That sunny morning, Grandma Lillie Willis walked to Longleaf Baptist Church with her three sons, Julian Willis, my Daddy, age nine, and his two brothers, Uncle Howard Willis, age thirteen, and Uncle Herman Willis, age eight. Grandma was never late to anything, especially church.

The message that morning was "Hell Fire and Brimstone." No, not at Longleaf Baptist, but at the Blackman Settlement.

Rapides Parish Deputy Sheriff John Franklin "Frank" Phillips and his posse approached William Blackman's cabin to arrest and charge him for violating the prohibition laws against bootlegging.

As the posse surrounded the cabin, Deputy Frank Phillips knocked on the front door and announced the reason for their official visit. A shotgun blast from inside hit Frank Phillips. Newspaper accounts said Deputy Phillips returned fire, killing William Blackman before he died.

Deputy Sheriff John Franklin "Frank" Phillips

Frank Phillips

One account said, "A community furor ensued over the much-beloved deputy's death, and a mob burned down the houses in the Blackman Settlement." They burned everything that would burn to ashes.

The senseless murder of the 38-year-old deputy who left behind a wife and three children enraged the entire community, Rapides Parish, and the great state of Louisiana. Among that group was my family, including Grandpa.

William Blackman's older brothers, "for their safety," were arrested, although they were not there that day. Later, a

307

Blackman family member said the "probable cause" was that they were brothers to William Blackman.

The Blackman brothers were not booked in Rapides Parish but "for their safety" in the nearby Vernon Parish Jail. After a short time, the Vernon Parish sheriff no longer wanted to be responsible for protecting them.

The Rapides Parish Sheriff sent three deputies to the Vernon Parish Jail in Leesville to take custody of the Blackman brothers and to transport them to Shreveport.

However, the deputies did not escort the brothers north from Leesville to Shreveport; instead, they chose a longer route back through Rapides Parish.

Somehow, a mob found out about this unusual route. As the deputies approached the horde on a back road in Rapides Parish, the road was blocked with vehicles. The deputies were told to "Move on," which they did, but not until the mob removed the Blackman Brothers from the three deputies' transport.

There, on the side of the road where all could later view, the mob lynched the brothers from a tree and riddled their bodies with bullets.

As the news spread like wildfire, much of America was outraged.

"Southern white federal officeholders repeatedly blocked anti-lynching legislation over the decades of the early 20th century, asserting that a federal role in thwarting lynching would violate 'state's rights.'"

The Ole Willis Home Place Longleaf, Louisiana, 1906

A little over a decade after the lynching, Grandpa died of alcoholism at age 54. The moonshine had eaten a hole in his stomach. The official cause of death was "stomach cancer."

As a nine-year-old boy, Daddy would hear this story told repeatedly, embellished with arrogance, hate, and pride, but never by our family.

Strange how one event will harden one man's heart and melt another.

But there was yet another tragedy that would soon be written on the tablets of Daddy's heart as a teenager.

As a child and teenager growing up in the Deep South, Daddy often encountered racial prejudice. Bigotry was a way of life to many. But the lynching after the Blackman Settlement incident and a chance encounter would forever change Daddy's heart concerning inequality.

One day, Daddy and his father, Randall "Rand" Willis, drove to Bob Johnson's Grocery Store at Shady Nook, near Longleaf, to buy gas.

A group of men my grandfather knew were laughing and motioned for Daddy and Grandpa to join them. Daddy was barely in his teens. As he stood mesmerized, the men spoke of an event the day before.

A black man had been arrested for inappropriate behavior towards a white woman. Some claimed much more, although there was no evidence, just rumors.

The exact details were not precise to Daddy. The black man was arrested. According to the men talking, the black man tried to escape on the 20-plus-mile trip to Alexandria's jail. The black man was shot repeatedly and died.

As the men laughed, it was clear even to a young boy this is what happens when a black man dares cross their bigoted code of behavior, which included a black man looking at a white woman inappropriately.

Daddy never forgot it and vowed that when he grew up, if he had his way, this would never happen again. One might think he was admired for this. On the contrary, he was despised as he began to speak against prejudice, not just for people of color, but for veterans and underprivileged, equal pay for women, and dozens of other causes until his death.

In a strange twist of fate, I met a woman in 1972 in Baton Rouge. She asked me how I liked Louisiana during my stay since I was from Texas. I told her, and in closing, I said, "I lived in Louisiana as a boy in a tiny village called Longleaf."

She teared up and said, "My father was killed there. He was a Deputy serving a warrant in the woods." Her father was Deputy John Franklin "Frank" Phillips.

His headstone in Glenmora, Louisiana, near Longleaf, reads, "He gave his life that others may live."

☆　　☆　　☆

After World War II, Daddy championed civil rights, which cost him the respect of many. He even took up an impossible cause from the 1940s to the 1990s: equal pay for women.

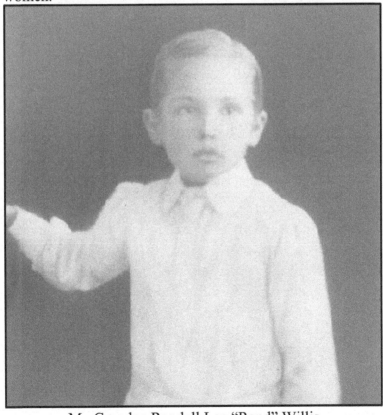

My Grandpa Randall Lee "Rand" Willis

My Grandpa Randall Lee "Rand" Willis

Daddy's mother and my grandmother, Lillie Hanks Willis. She married my grandfather and namesake, Randall Lee "Rand" Willis, on January 11, 1914. She was only 16. Daddy carried this photo during WW II.

For Randy Willis ~

a hero for Children's Hospital and
for our family. your wisdom and
your grace are our blessings.
With generations of gratitude ~

Wildflowers
Across America

Lady Bird Johnson

Luci Baines Johnson

Nicole Nugent Covert

I first met Lady Bird Johnson at a Darrell Royal pickin' party at his home on Onion Creek south of Austin.

I last saw Lady Bird Johnson at the Headliners Club in Austin. As always, she was escorted by two Secret Service Agents.

She had her book *Wildflowers Across America* hand-delivered to me at my home in Austin. This inscription is on the inside cover of her book and reads:

"For Randy Willis

"A hero for Children's Hospital and for our family. Your wisdom and your grace are our blessings.

"With generations of gratitude."

Lady Bird Johnson
Luci Baines Johnson (Lady Bird's Daughter)
Nicole Nugent Covert (Lady Bird's Granddaughter)

Wildflowers Across America —Lady Bird Johnson

I first met Lady Bird Johnson at Darrell Royal's home. Her late husband, Lyndon Johnson, was close friends with Coach Royal.

315

I met Coach Darrell Royal in 1976. He picked Johnny Rodriguez and me up at the Sheraton Crest Hotel (today, The LINE Austin). Country singer Moe Bandy was with him. Coach Royal drove us to his home at 1200 Belmont Parkway on Shoal Creek by way of the new Austin highway, MoPac. The first six miles had opened the year before.

We arrived at Coach Royal's home on Belmont Parkway within minutes. His home on Belmont Parkway and later Onion Creek were the sites of many great pickin' parties. Later, I hosted many pickin' parties at my Austin home. Coach Royal never missed one.

Randy Willis and Darrell Royal

THE WHITE HOUSE

WASHINGTON

June 12, 2003

Mr. Randy Willis
Post Office Box 15345
Austin, Texas 78761-5345

Dear Mr. Willis:

Thank you for your kind words of support and for remembering me in
your prayers.

At this time of great consequence for our Nation, I am honored to lead our
country. We pray for the safety of the men and women who serve around
the world to defend our freedom. We also pray for God's peace in the
affairs of men. And we thank God for our Nation's many blessings. I
appreciate knowing that I can count on your support as my Administration
continues to work on issues that are important to Americans.

Laura joins me in sending our best wishes.

Sincerely,

George W. Bush

George W. Bush, 43rd President of the United States.

A generation later, after moving to Texas, our family
returned for one of our many visits to our old homeplace near
Longleaf.

Like Daddy, I was a boy, too, when I first experienced
racial prejudice cloaked in tradition. We drove from our old

317

home place to Glenmora to visit a friend of Daddy's from high school whom he had not seen in many years.

Daddy's views on civil rights and segregation had returned to Louisiana by then. Daddy's "old friend" Charlie (not his real name) did not invite us inside.

As we stood in Charlie's front yard, he shared what he described as an event he had witnessed the week before that made him sick to his stomach. "Julian, I saw a white man shake hands with a (racial slur)," Charlie said, waiting for Daddy's response.

"Have you ever heard of such a thing?" Daddy did not respond, and we quickly left. We never returned.

☆   ☆   ☆

Years before, Daddy was inspired by Hubert H. Humphrey's speech supporting civil rights before the Democratic National Convention in 1948. Humphrey was mayor of Minneapolis and a candidate for Senate.

The entire Mississippi delegation and half the Alabama contingent walked out of the convention.

Nearly two weeks after the convention, President Truman issued executive orders mandating equal opportunity in the armed forces and the federal civil service. Daddy agreed with Truman.

Later, Martin Luther King Jr. influenced Daddy even further. Daddy admired Republican Margaret Chase Smith, too. She was the first senator to stand up against Joseph McCarthy's Red Scare.

However, his support of Lyndon Johnson's landmark legislation would rival his admiration of Franklin Delano Roosevelt's leadership during World War II, two decades before.

Daddy showed respect to those who had different political views. He once had a private meeting with a local doctor named Ron Paul, who was considering entering politics. Daddy told me, "I don't agree with hardly anything he said, but I believe he is honest. Well, I believe he believes what he's saying."

Politics was not the central theme of Daddy's life. Nor was it the driving force behind his decisions. His beliefs could be summed up in two words: honesty and character. Yet, those beliefs were exemplified by a politician, John Adams.

The second president of the United States was John Adams. He was the first to reside at the White House after the nation's capital moved to Washington.

On November 2, 1800—his second night in the new building Adams wrote in a letter to his wife, Abigail Adams:

"Before I end my Letter I pray Heaven to bestow the best of Blessings on this House and all that shall hereafter inhabit it. May none but honest and wise Men ever rule under this roof."

In 1945, the final year of World War II, President Franklin D. Roosevelt had that blessing carved into the State Dining Room fireplace mantel.

John F. Kennedy's administration commissioned a new mantel with John Adam's words intact.

Children's
Hospital Foundation
of Austin

Mr. Randy Willis

P.O. Box 270248
Austin, TX 78748

Dear Mr. Willis,

On behalf of the Board of Trustees of the Children's Hospital Foundation, thank you for your gift of $50,000.00 to the Children's Hospital of Austin.

Since 1988, Children's Hospital has provided the best pediatric care available to all children in our community. Your generosity assures the continued excellence in healthcare at Children's Hospital and assists with the exciting expansion efforts currently underway.

Thank you again for your support. Your gift is building a *brighter* future for the children of Central Texas.

Sincerely,

Missy

Maureen (Missy) Wood
Executive Director

Thanks for everything Randy! We are so thrilled!

P.S. *In compliance with IRS regulation, this letter serves as verification that you received no goods or services in consideration of your contribution. Your gift is deductible to the extent allowed by law.*

320

Children's
Hospital Foundation
of Austin

February 20, 2003

Mr. Randy Willis
PO Box 15345
Austin, TX 78761

Dear Mr. Willis,

On behalf of Children's Hospital of Austin, thank you for your most generous support of
the 2003 Children's Hospital of Austin's Gala *"Celebre la Vida"*. **Thanks to an
outpouring of support from our community, we are proud to announce that the net
proceeds from this event are a record breaking $363,000!**

These funds will go towards medical equipment advancements at Children's Hospital of
Austin. Specifically, anesthesia and surgical equipment is very dependent upon electronics
and computers. As current technology evolves and new opportunities emerge, Children's
Hospital of Austin is fortunate to be able to stand at the forefront of cutting edge high tech
thanks to your support.

Much appreciation goes to the hard work and dedication of this year's Gala chairs, Dr.
Pierre and Angela Filardi. Thanks to the many hours shared by them and their outstanding
committee, this event will make a significant impact on each and every patient served at
Children's Hospital of Austin.

We look forward to sharing another year of celebration with you on January 24, 2004
under the leadership of chairs Jill and Jon Conant. Thank you again for your generosity, it
will help make miracles happen in the life of a child.

Sincerely,

Missy

Maureen "Missy" Wood
Executive Director

*Randy — Thank you
so much for your
sponsorship of this event!*
😊

November 30, 2004

Mr. Randy Willis
P. O. Box 15345
Austin, Texas 78761-5345

Dear Mr. Willis:

Because you gave so generously to the University during our seven-year *We're Texas* capital campaign, you played a key role in its success. I thank you for your dedication and your support.

Enclosed is a booklet we have put together to share highlights of the campaign. It would take many more pages than these to convey the full impact of the campaign on our students, faculty, and programs. However, I hope that this overview gives you an idea of how your contribution has strengthened The University of Texas at Austin and helped shape our future.

The University is deeply grateful for your generosity.

Sincerely,

Larry R. Faulkner
President

Enclosure

☆   ☆   ☆

APPENDIX E
SUBJECT TO CHANGE–SOON

I write at my home in the Texas Hill Country and only two other places, one on a beach and one in the mountains. All three have spectacular views.

Of the three, I only write in bed in Costa Rica. Writing in Costa Rica, overlooking Pan Dulce Beach, with the sounds of the Pacific Ocean and Scarlet Macaws feeding in the trees.

Squirrel Monkeys jump and play, and I marvel at the ingenuity of clever White-faced Capuchin Monkeys. Spider Monkeys swing gracefully through the trees with long arms, legs, and tails. And the haunting call of Howler Monkeys.

I love the view of the Pacific Ocean coastline through the rugged rainforest as the sunsets.

My view overlooks Pan Dulce Beach in Costa Rica.

☆   ☆   ☆

Yet there is a fourth view I long to see. My favorite author lived there as a boy but never wrote a book like me. How strange, I know. He was born in a little-known town like me. His family moved to another small community like mine in the Texas Hill Country.

He never owned a home like me. He never went to college like me. Unlike me, he never traveled more than a hundred miles or so.

Many of his friends betrayed him. We've all been there, I know. The religious folks didn't like Him. Perhaps it was because He was homeless and dressed far below their standards, I don't know. Few understand him. I reckon the deck was stacked against him initially, but he could write like none other.

He once wrote a few words in the sand. Those words seemed to apply to everyone. Go figure. That was a creative writing class that I wish I had attended. But oh, I have numerous times since.

He wrote my name once on a hot August night. It was the 24th day in the year of our Lord, 1958.

That night, he wrote not on paper but on a tablet of flesh, my heart with ink, His blood. At times, it seemed he had written on a stone tablet. The ink seems to have faded with my choices, but oh no, thanks to Him, not me, it is permanently written in red.

As a boy, He must have often stared across the valley to the land far below. A land He will return to sooner than later. He's booked my reservation, first class, I'm told. He's paid my fair in total, although I sometimes take credit.

At age twelve, The boy once walked across the valley with a view toward a city called Jerusalem. The occasion was the Festival of Passover. Many say Passover is but a picture of Him with crosses; I've been told three. He will be nailed to the center one, which is meant for me, I know, the guilty one, not He.

This year was different. The boy became separated from his Mother and Stepfather. They were gravely concerned; He scarcely cared. After three days, they found him in His Father's house, sitting among teachers, listening ever so carefully and asking questions no one dared ask. He spoke with authority far beyond his years, which amazed them.

When they return home to a tiny village called Nazareth, I've often wondered how he viewed the valley below. It's known as Mount Precipice today and is located just outside his home, with panoramic views that only He can see.

It is believed by some to be the site of the Rejection of Him described by Dr. Luke in his Book of Good News. According to the old story, the people of his hometown, not accepting Him as Messiah, tried to push him from the mountain, but "He passed through the midst of them and went away."

That sounds familiar to me, for I see it every day. Be assured many have tried, and many more believe they can.

What were his thoughts as he gazed at the Jezreel Valley below, which will take center stage in a battle some call Armageddon? The final battle between the forces of Light, directed by Him, and darkness, led by His foe.

He will not come this time as a baby laid in a feed trough called a manger because no one has room for Him, much like today. Nor will he come as a man who angered everyone in the synagogue as he read from the scroll of Isaiah, "Today, as you listen, this Scripture has been fulfilled."

325

Nor will he come as a man to be beaten, mocked, spit upon, and nailed to a tree. This time, He will come as King of kings and the Lord of lords; every tongue will confess Him, and every knee will bow.

His name is Jesus, above all names, and He is coming again. I will be with Him, and you will be too if you know Him as Lord and Savior. All the angels in Heaven, which are innumerable, will be with Him. The Saints of all ages will be with Him, too.

What a view that will be that day when He comes again, this time riding a White Steed cloaked in His Divine Glory for all the world to see.

He speaks but two words to the fallen angel Lucifer, known as Satan these days, "Drop dead," some Biblical scholars say. I'm so thankful I'll witness that, for he has been my enemy for too long.

As I examine the evidence and sum up Christ Jesus' influence, I must conclude that all the writers who have ever written have not influenced humankind like the Author of authors.

He once said, "My kingdom is not of this world," but that is subject to change—soon!

Say yes to Christ—today. You will never regret that decision. And be ready for a view like none other when He comes again with you and me, I pray.

The view from my Texas Hill Country home.

The view of the sky slopes Keystone, Colorado.

The view Jesus saw as a boy. Believed to be the site of the Rejection of Jesus described in the Gospel of Luke. They tried to push him from the mountain known as Mount Precipice today, which is located near Nazareth.

In Appreciation

I'm thankful to the many people who encouraged me to write about our family's history. My first cousin, Donnie Willis, planted the first seed in my mind to write about our 4th Great-Grandfather, Joseph Willis. Donnie has been pastor of Fenton Baptist Church in Fenton, Louisiana, for over 50 years.

I'm also thankful to my sainted grandmother, Lillie Hanks Willis. She had a treasure chest of stories about Joseph Willis and insisted I write them down.

My Uncle Howard Willis was our family's master storyteller when I was younger. I sat for many hours, mesmerized by him. His granddaughter and my cousin Kimberly Willis Holt were inspired by him, too. She is a National Book Award Winner and author of *When Zachary Beaver Came to Town*, *My Louisiana Sky*, and the *Piper Reed* series. *When Zachary Beaver Came to Town*, *My Louisiana Sky* were adapted as films of the same name.

I'm thankful to my late cousin and the maternal great-grandson of Joseph Willis, Dr. Greene Wallace Strother. His Uncle Polk Willis and Aunt Olive Willis tended to Joseph Willis in his final years, and they shared all that Joseph told them. Dr. Strother gave me his extensive research in 1980. He served as chaplain to General Claire Chennault's "Flying Tigers" while in China as a missionary. He was a Southern Baptist missionary emeritus to China and Malaysia.

Karon McCartney, Archivist at the Louisiana Baptist Convention, has provided much help in organizing, cataloging, and protecting my research for decades at the Louisiana Baptist Building in Alexandria.

329

My fellow historian and friend, the late Dr. Sue Eakin, asked me if I would help her research William Prince Ford. I learned much about William Prince Ford and Solomon Northup and their relationship with Joseph Willis from her. She encouraged me to have my research adapted into a play.

The play is entitled *Twice a Slave* and is based on my novel of the same name. My books *Three Winds Blowing* and *Destiny* are partly based on the relationship of Joseph Willis with William Prince Ford and Solomon Northup.

Dr. Eakin is best known for documenting, annotating, and reviving interest in Solomon Northup's 1853 book *Twelve Years a Slave*. At eighteen, she rediscovered a long-forgotten copy of Solomon Northup's book on the shelves of a bookstore near the LSU campus in Baton Rouge. The bookstore owner sold it to her for only 25 cents.

In 2013, *12 Years a Slave* won the Academy Award for Best Picture. In his acceptance speech for the honor, director Steve McQueen thanked Dr. Eakin: "I'd like to thank this amazing historian, Sue Eakin, whose life she gave her life's work to preserving Solomon's book."

I am thankful for my three sons: Aaron Willis, Joshua Willis, and Adam Willis. Their strength of character has been demonstrated many times in how they treat those who can do nothing for them. The responses of the character Jimbo in four of my novels inspired me.

And above all, I am thankful to the Good Lord. He has given me wells I did not dig and vineyards I did not plant.

—Randy Willis 2024

About the Author

Randy Willis is as much at home in the saddle as he is in front of the computer, where he composes his family sagas.

Drawing on his family heritage of explorers, settlers, soldiers, cowboys, and pastors, Randy carries on the tradition of loving the outdoors and sharing it in the adventures he creates for readers of his novels. He is the author of two biographies and his new memoir, *To the Best of My Recollection.*

He is also the author of *Destiny, Beckoning Candle, Twice a Slave, Three Winds Blowing, Texas Wind, Louisiana Wind, The Apostle to the Opelousas, The Story of Joseph Willis, To the Best of My Recollection,* and many published articles.

Four bestselling authors' books, including Randy Willis's *Twice a Slave,* have been chosen as a Jerry B. Jenkins Select Book. Jerry Jenkins is a 21-time New York Times bestselling author. He is the author of more than 200 books, with sales of more than 70 million copies of the best-selling *Left Behind* series.

Twice a Slave has been adapted into a dramatic play by Dr. D. "Pete" Richardson (Associate Professor of Theater at Louisiana Christian University).

He owns Randy Willis Music Publishing (an ASCAP-affiliated music publishing company) and Town Lake Music Publishing, LLC (a BMI-affiliated music publishing company). He is an ASCAP-affiliated songwriter. He is a rancher in the Texas Hill Country.

Randy Willis founded Operation Warm Heart, which feeds and clothes those in need in Central Texas. He was a member of the Board of Directors of Our Mission Possible (empowering at-risk teens to discover their greatness) in Austin, Texas.

Randy Willis was a charter member of the Board of Trustees of the Joseph Willis Institute for Great Awakening Studies at Louisiana College (Louisiana Christian University today).

Randy Willis was born in Oakdale, Louisiana, and lived as a child near Longleaf, Louisiana, and Barber Creek. His parents, Julian "Jake" and Ruth Willis, moved to Clute, Texas, when he was four and Angleton, Texas, when he was ten.

He graduated from Angleton High School in Angleton, Texas, and Texas State University in San Marcos, Texas. He was a graduate student at Texas State University for six years. He is the father of three sons and has six grandchildren.

He resides near his three sons and their families in the Texas Hill Country.

Randy Willis is the fourth great-grandson of Reverend Joseph Willis, the first Protestant preacher west of the Mississippi River and his foremost historian.

332

Darrell Royal, Willie Nelson, and Randy Willis
Telling Stories Writing Songs
By Kathleen Hudson
Published by University of Texas Press

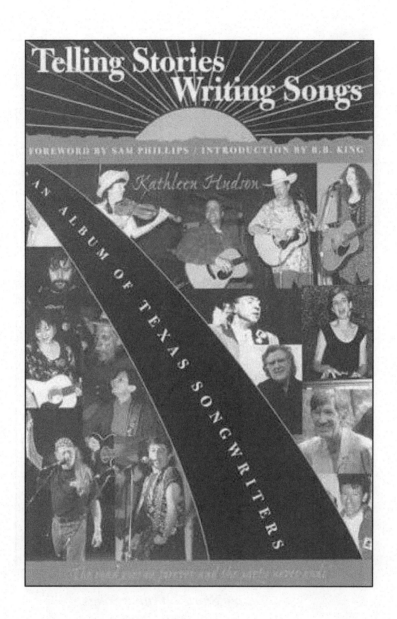

Telling Stories Writing Songs

FOREWORD BY SAM PHILLIPS / INTRODUCTION BY B.B. KING

Kathleen Hudson

AN ALBUM OF TEXAS SONGWRITERS

"Riding fences" in my red GMC pickup.

When the horses, longhorn cattle, and grandkids are fed, I reckon I can go home and write a paragraph or two about these three Texas legends and "One" other.

335

Olivia Grace Willis's Kiger Mustangs

Olivia Willis and Josh Willis

Adam Willis

337

Presley Willis and Aaron Willis

Baylee Willis

Juliette Willis, age two on Liberty

Corbin Willis (16) at Kobe Steak House & Sushi.

My Three Sons
They have blessed me.

Adam Willis, Aaron Willis, Josh Willis

Adam, Aaron, and Josh Willis on "Big Boy."

Aaron, Josh, and Adam Willis.
The Blanco River Wimberley, Texas

Josh, Aaron, and Adam Willis headed with me to
Hyde Park Baptist Church in Austin, Texas.

Aaron, Josh, Randy, and Adam Willis
Snowmobiling Summit County, Colorado

Adam, Josh, and Aaron Willis
Rainbow in the background.
Royal Gorge Bridge Cañon City, Colorado

The Louvre Art Museum, Paris, France.
Adam Willis, Josh Willis, and Aaron Willis

Arapahoe Basin, Colorado. Over 13,000 feet.
Josh Willis, Aaron Willis, Adam Willis

Adam Willis (the baby), Randy Willis, Josh Willis, and Aaron Willis hiking in the national forest above our home near Westcliffe, Colorado, in the Sangre de Cristo Mountains.

White Water Rafting the Snake River South of Jackson Hole, Wyoming. Josh and Aaron are back left, I am in the red striped shirt, and Adam is below smiling.

Josh Willis, Adam Willis, Aaron Willis

Josh Willis, Adam Willis, and Aaron Willis
Deep Sea Fishing Acapulco, Mexico

Adam Willis Rome, Italy

Josh Willis Maui, Hawaii

Josh Willis Costa Rica Pan Dulce Beach

350

Aaron Willis
The National Gallery art museum in Trafalgar Square
in Westminster, Central London, England.

My three sons, Adam, Aaron, and Josh Willis.
Notre-Dame de Paris

A note my son Aaron Willis handed me the night of his
Wimberley High School Graduation.

353

My Inspiration to Write

A man's character is measured by what it takes to discourage him. Talent, wealth, position, and fame will fade like the autumn colors, but his character will remain for generations yet to come. — Randy Willis 2024

In 1758, Joseph Willis was born a Cherokee slave to his father.

His father died when he was only 18. His uncle then cheats him out of his inheritance, which would have made him one of the wealthiest men in North Carolina.

Seven years later, he married Rachel Bradford. After having four children, she died in childbirth in 1794. She was only 32.

He seeks ordination from his local Baptist church. He was denied. Their reason was "the cause of Christ would suffer." His dark skin was the issue. No one would respond to an "inferior" person of color. The first slaves were Indians in North and South Carolina.

He marries again. Sarah was her name, an Irish orphan. After having two children, she died in 1798.

He is 40. In 1798, he had a 50% chance of living to 50. He has been cheated out of his inheritance, lost two wives, denied ordination, and is alone with six children. He once felt called by God. He now feels he was wrong. His life is almost over. He gives up.

That is until an encounter soon with the Holy Spirit. In his 90s, he passed this story down to his grandchildren but only would say he prayed he could have that same encounter with the Lord again. It never happened. But, from then on, he was on a mission to go where no others would dare.

In the Spring, Joseph Willis and others left South Carolina in 1798 and traveled by land to the northeastern corner of Tennessee, to the banks of the Holston River.

There, they built flatboats, and when the Holston River reached sufficient depth toward the end of that year, they set out for the Natchez country of Mississippi by way of the Holston, Tennessee, Ohio, and Mississippi Rivers.

When they reached the confluence of the Tennessee River and the Clinch River (near present-day Kingston, Tennessee), they were attacked by the Cherokee.

Joseph, being half-Cherokee with swarthy skin, has knowledge of his Cherokee mother's language. It would save their lives.

Within months, he entered the hostile Spanish-controlled Louisiana Territory when the dreaded Code Noir was the law of the land by swimming the mighty Mississippi riding only a mule.

The penalty was death. The local religious folks attempt to kill him numerous times.

Joseph moves from very dangerous to insanely dangerous.

355

His skin color and understanding of the Cherokee language would again save his life when he crossed the Calcasieu River into "No Man's Land" as the first Protestant preacher to dare do so.

There were no laws. No country wanted it. Joseph would find other Cherokee and indigenous people, outlaws from Texas. Runaway slaves from the New Orleans slave markets and the Mississippi River slave transports. And the Pirate Jean Lafitte. The mission field was tailor-made for the outcast preacher of Jesus.

Joseph Willis lived to 96, establishing over 20 churches in Mississippi and Louisiana. Today, over 2,000 churches have sprung from the seeds he planted.

☆　　☆　　☆

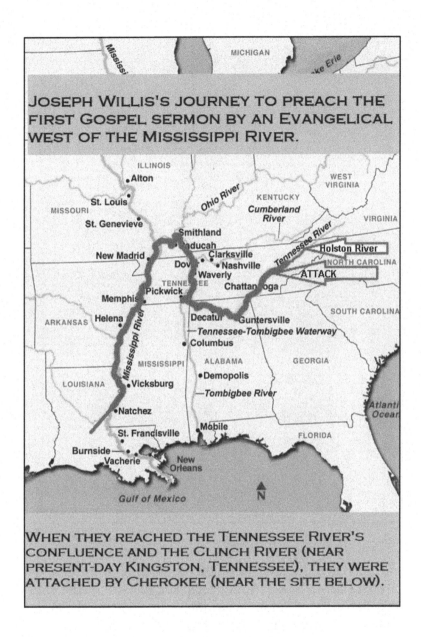

JOSEPH WILLIS'S JOURNEY TO PREACH THE FIRST GOSPEL SERMON BY AN EVANGELICAL WEST OF THE MISSISSIPPI RIVER.

WHEN THEY REACHED THE TENNESSEE RIVER'S CONFLUENCE AND THE CLINCH RIVER (NEAR PRESENT-DAY KINGSTON, TENNESSEE), THEY WERE ATTACHED BY CHEROKEE (NEAR THE SITE BELOW).

357

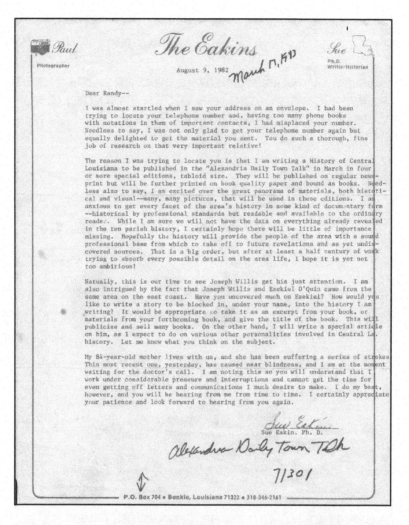

The Eakins

Paul
Photographer

August 9, 1982   March 17, 1985

Sue
Ph.D.
Writer/Historian

Dear Randy--

I was almost startled when I saw your address on an envelope. I had been trying to locate your telephone number and, having too many phone books with notations in them of important contacts, I had misplaced your number. Needless to say, I was not only glad to get your telephone number again but equally delighted to get the material you sent. You do such a thorough, fine job of research on that very important relative!

The reason I was trying to locate you is that I am writing a History of Central Louisiana to be published in the "Alexandria Daily Town Talk" in March in four or more special editions, tabloid size. They will be published on regular news-print but will be further printed on book quality paper and bound as books. Needless also to say, I am excited over the great panorama of materials, both historical and visual--many, many pictures, that will be used in these editions. I am anxious to get every facet of the area's history in some kind of documentary form --historical by professional standards but readable and available to the ordinary reader. While I am sure we will not have the data on everything already revealed in the ten parish history, I certainly hope there will be little of importance missing. Hopefully the history will provide the people of the area with a sound professional base from which to take off to future revelations and as yet undiscovered sources. That is a big order, but after at least a half century of work trying to absorb every possible detail on the area life, I hope it is yet not too ambitious!

Natually, this is our time to see Joseph Willis get his just attention. I am also intrigued by the fact that Joseph Willis and Ezekiel O'Quin came from the same area on the east coast. Have you uncovered much on Ezekiel? How would you like to write a story to be blocked in, under your name, into the history I am writing? It would be appropriate to take it as an excerpt from your book, or materials from your forthcoming book, and give the title of the book. This will publicize and sell many books. On the other hand, I will write a special article on him, as I expect to do on various other personalities involved in Central La. history. Let me know what you think on the subject.

My 84-year-old mother lives with us, and she has been suffering a series of strokes. This most recent one, yesterday, has caused near blindness, and I am at the moment waiting for the doctor's call. I am noting this so you will understand that I work under considerable pressure and interruptions and cannot get the time for even getting off letters and communications I much desire to make. I do my best, however, and you will be hearing from me from time to time. I certainly appreciate your patience and look forward to hearing from you again.

Sue Eakin
Sue Eakin, Ph. D.

Alexandria Daily Town Talk

7/301

P.O. Box 704 • Bunkie, Louisiana 71322 • 318-346-2161

Dr. Eakin is best known for documenting, annotating, and reviving interest in Solomon Northup's 1853 book *Twelve Years a Slave*. At eighteen, she rediscovered a long-forgotten copy of Solomon Northup's book on the shelves of a bookstore near the LSU campus in Baton Rouge. The bookstore owner sold it to her for only 25 cents.

In 2013, *12 Years a Slave* won the Academy Award for Best Picture. In his acceptance speech for the honor, director Steve McQueen thanked Dr. Eakin: "I'd like to thank this amazing historian, Sue Eakin, whose life she gave her life's work to preserving Solomon's book."

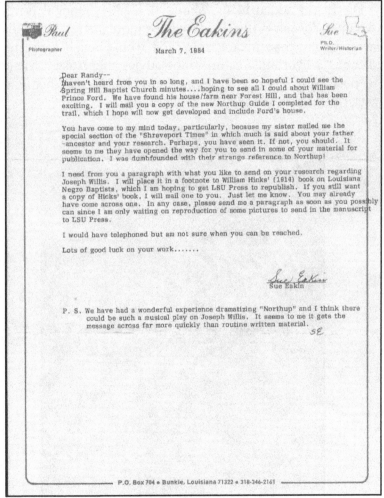

Paul   **The Eakins**   *Sue*

Photographer   March 7, 1984   Ph.D.
Writer/Historian

Dear Randy--
I haven't heard from you in so long, and I have been so hopeful I could see the Spring Hill Baptist Church minutes....hoping to see all I could about William Prince Ford. We have found his house/farm near Forest Hill, and that has been exciting. I will mail you a copy of the new Northup Guide I completed for the trail, which I hope will now get developed and include Ford's house.

You have come to my mind today, particularly, because my sister mailed me the special section of the "Shreveport Times" in which much is said about your father -ancestor and your research. Perhaps, you have seen it. If not, you should. It seems to me they have opened the way for you to send in some of your material for publication. I was dumbfounded with their strange reference to Northup!

I need from you a paragraph with what you like to send on your research regarding Joseph Willis. I will place it in a footnote to William Hicks' (1914) book on Louisiana Negro Baptists, which I am hoping to get LSU Press to republish. If you still want a copy of Hicks' book, I will mail one to you. Just let me know. You may already have come across one. In any case, please send me a paragraph as soon as you possibly can since I am only waiting on reproduction of some pictures to send in the manuscript to LSU Press.

I would have telephoned but am not sure when you can be reached.

Lots of good luck on your work.......

Sue Eakin
Sue Eakin

P. S. We have had a wonderful experience dramatizing "Northup" and I think there could be such a musical play on Joseph Willis. It seems to me it gets the message across far more quickly than routine written material.
       SE

P.O. Box 704 • Bunkie, Louisiana 71322 • 318-346-2161

This P.S. above is why I had my novel *Twice a Slave* adapted into a play.

Dr. Eakin wrote me on March 7, 1984, in the P.S. above, "We had a wonderful experience dramatizing Northup, and I think there could be a musical play on Joseph Willis. It seems to me it gets the message across far more quickly than routine written material."

Dr. Eakin added in the above P.S., "A fictional novel based upon Joseph Willis' life would be more interesting to the general public than a biography and would reach a greater audience." Never underestimate the advice of a trusted friend in a postscript. I wrote *Twice a Slave* because of her P.S. (postscript). Then, the play.

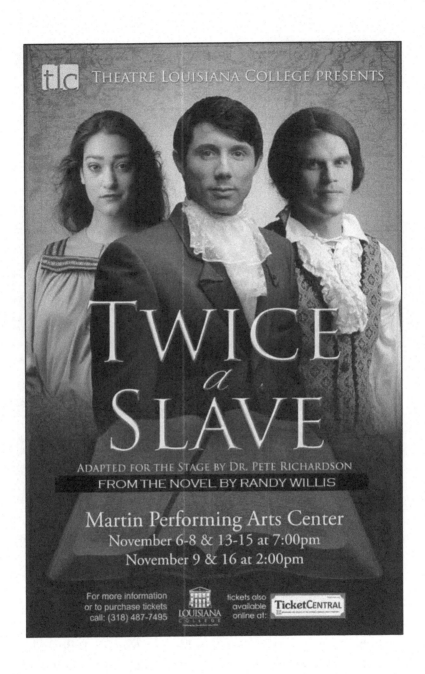

TWICE a SLAVE

ADAPTED FOR THE STAGE BY DR. PETE RICHARDSON
FROM THE NOVEL BY RANDY WILLIS

Martin Performing Arts Center
November 6-8 & 13-15 at 7:00pm
November 9 & 16 at 2:00pm

For more information
or to purchase tickets
call: (318) 487-7495

LOUISIANA
COLLEGE

tickets also
available
online at:

TicketCENTRAL

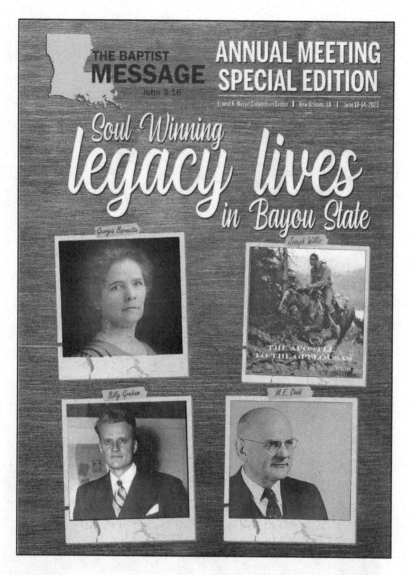

THE BAPTIST MESSAGE
John 3:16

ANNUAL MEETING SPECIAL EDITION

Ernest N. Morial Convention Center | New Orleans, LA | June 10-14, 2023

Soul Winning legacy lives in Bayou State

Georgia Barnette

Joseph Willis

THE APOSTLE TO THE OPELOUSAS
By Randy Willis

Billy Graham

M.E. Dodd

I would later receive excellent advice from incredible writers. Coach Darrell Royal introduced me to James Michener. My favorite book of his was *Hawaii*, followed by *Centennial* and, of course, *Texas*. All three were adapted into movies.

Randy Willis, JR, James Michener, Darrell Royal

I first met Michener's friend, H.C. Carter, at Austin Baptist Church in Austin. He invited me to lunch with his wife and former Austin Mayor Ron Mullen. He was a founding member of the Texas Longhorn Breeders Association.

I love Longhorn Cattle and Kiger Mustangs. I bought two Kiger Mustangs for my granddaughter, Olivia Grace Willis. She's a nine-year-old cowgirl.

H.C. Carter raised Longhorn Cattle near Dripping Springs, only 30 minutes from where Olivia's Mustangs are.

H.C.'s knowledge of Longhorn Cattle was of keen interest to James Michener and later influenced my novels *Texas Wind* and *Louisiana Wind*. While James Michener gathered the information for his epic book *Texas*, he spent

363

many hours with H.C. discussing cattle drives and Texas history on H.C.'s front porch in Dripping Springs and my home.

Michener gave H.C. more acknowledgments in his book *Texas* than any other source. Michener told H.C., "Carter if this book is a failure, it's your fault."

James Michener became a philanthropist, donating more than $100 million to educational, cultural, and writing institutions, including $37 million to the University of Texas. Michener lived his final years in Austin and endowed the Mitchener Center for Writers at the University of Texas.

★ ★ ★

Randy Willis

Vaya con Dios, Randy Willis

Published by:
American Writers Publishing, LLC
PO Box 111
Wimberley, Texas 78676

512-565-0161
randywillisnovelist@gmail.com
www.threewindsblowing.com